Praise for *The Medic:*
Life and Death in the Last Days of WWII

"[A] book that should be given to every schoolboy in the country at the age of thirteen. . . . *The Medic*, which teaches us so much, makes clear that sometimes the monsters in war are not only the enemy."
—Gloria Emerson, *Los Angeles Times Book Review*

"[*The Medic*] has all the unadorned honesty of a good war letter home . . . with clear, clean prose, suctioned free of all self-indulgence . . . this brief but important book speaks to us with all the authority of letters from a father long gone."
—*San Francisco Chronicle*

"This brutal and yet frequently uplifting saga of war has the ring of authenticity. There are no 'good guys' or 'bad guys' here, although the presence of both good and evil is constant. This is a disturbing, revealing, and very important glimpse of warfare at the most elementary level."
—*Booklist*

"Powerful interludes about time as a World War II medic, sleeping in freezing trenches, dodging bullets, treating devastating wounds."
—*San Francisco* magazine

"If you read any war book this year, read Leo Litwak's short tale of his actual experiences as a combat medic in World War II. Litwak's story is simple and told without embellishment. Each sentence carries the astounding ring of truth. Litwak is simply a master of observation."
—*Decatur Daily*

"An unsentimental WWII memoir . . . an unflinching portrait of the times."   —*Kirkus Reviews*

"Litwak's tough-minded narrative portrays war's peculiar customs with compelling honesty and wry humor."
—*Publishers Weekly*

"A remembrance . . . of normal young men who were put in extraordinary circumstances and lived to tell about it. Spare . . . strong and vivid."   —*The Denver Post*

PENGUIN BOOKS

THE MEDIC

Leo Litwak grew up in Detroit and served in World War II
as a medic. He taught English literature at San Francisco
State University for more than thirty years and is the author of the novels *Waiting for the News*, which won the
1970 National Jewish Book Award, and *To the Hanging
Gardens*. His short story "The Eleventh Edition" was
awarded first prize in the 1990 edition of *Prize Stories:
The O. Henry Awards*.

THE MEDIC

Life and Death in the Last Days of WWII

LEO LITWAK

PENGUIN BOOKS

PENGUIN BOOKS
Published by the Penguin Group
Penguin Putnam Inc., 375 Hudson Street,
New York, New York 10014, U.S.A.
Penguin Books Ltd, 80 Strand, London WC2R 0RL, England
Penguin Books Australia Ltd, 250 Camberwell Road,
Camberwell, Victoria 3124, Australia
Penguin Books Canada Ltd, 10 Alcorn Avenue,
Toronto, Ontario, Canada M4V 3B2
Penguin Books India (P) Ltd, 11 Community Centre,
Panchsheel Park, New Delhi – 110 017, India
Penguin Books (N.Z.) Ltd, Cnr Rosedale and Airborne Roads,
Albany, Auckland, New Zealand
Penguin Books (South Africa) (Pty) Ltd, 24 Sturdee Avenue,
Rosebank, Johannesburg 2196, South Africa

Penguin Books Ltd, Registered Offices:
Harmondsworth, Middlesex, England

First published in the United States of America by Algonquin Books
of Chapel Hill, a division of Workman Publishing 2001
Published in Penguin Books 2002

10 9 8 7 6 5 4 3 2 1

THE LIBRARY OF CONGRESS HAS CATALOGED
THE HARDCOVER EDITION AS FOLLOWS:
Litwak, Leo, 1924–
The medic : life and death in the last days of WWII / by Leo Litwak.
p.   cm.
ISBN 1-56512-305-0 (hc.)
ISBN 0 14 20.0219 4 (pbk.)
1. Litwak, Leo; 1924–   2. World War, 1939–1945—Personal narratives,
American.   3. United States. Army—Medical personnel—Biography.
4. World War, 1939–1945—Campaigns—Western Front.   I. Title.
D811.5 L559   2001
940.54'8173—dc21   00–068231

Printed in the United States of America
Set in Times New Roman

DEDICATIONS

To Jessica
To Emma
To Sophia
To Carolyn

ACKNOWLEDGMENTS

My thanks to Herbert Gold for his all-important counsel and close reading; to Charlotte Painter for her detailed critiques; to George and Annie Leonard for their support and fine editing; to Molly Giles for her sly, trenchant criticism; to Bernard Taper for suggesting Algonquin; to Tom Farber for his encouragement; to the men and women of the Saloon who urged me on; to my agent, Ellen Levine, who kept me on the path; to my editor, Duncan Murrell, who read the manuscript as I hoped it would be read and guided me to the finishing touches.

The Medic

In the last weeks of the war in Europe my company entered a village in Saxony that was decked out in white flags. We found cozy billets in large houses—feather beds, tile ovens in kitchens, cellars stocked with food and drink. Details were assigned, the night's password given, guards posted.

One of the guards outside our platoon billet heard a noise in nearby bushes, maybe ten yards away, spotted a German uniform, yelled something like, Who goes there! and started shooting before there could be an answer. I was the platoon medic and came running when I heard the call for aid. The German lay facedown, his hair, abundant, dirty yellow, was tangled in the bushes. We turned him over. He was a kid, maybe sixteen years old, unarmed and barely alive.

Maybe he didn't understand the challenge. Maybe he didn't have time to respond. The thirty-caliber bullets had scooped out his chest and bared his heart. When I recall the scene I see his beating heart. I don't know how that can be but that's how I remember it. He must have been prone when the bullets hit, just starting to rise, wedged into the bushes. He still had breath to whisper and I put my ear to his lips.

"Ich ergebe mich. Warum schiessen sie?" I surrender. Why do you shoot?

"Wir haben nicht gewüsst." We didn't know, I said, and uselessly bandaged him with large compresses and two-inch gauze and tape. The medics from the battalion aid station arrived by jeep and carried him away. The next day when I asked a medic from the aid station what happened to the kid he said it was a hopeless case; why had I bothered to send him back when he had no chance? I'd wasted the resources of the aid station and the field hospital.

Toward the end the German army was stocked with kids and old men, and this kid, among the masses of dead, was no one special. Kids were running the war. I wasn't much more than a kid myself. The wound was terrible but I'd seen worse. After we packed him off to the aid station I returned to a meal scrounged from a German cellar— ham and black bread and white wine and cherry preserves —and didn't give the dying boy much thought.

Twenty-three years later he unexpectedly showed up. It was 1967. I was at the Esalen Institute, on assignment for the *New York Times Magazine.* Esalen, on the Big Sur coast of California, bordered a wilderness preserve on one side. On the other side were steep cliffs and the Pacific Ocean. Between wilderness and ocean there were plush meadows and a lodge and cabins and hot mineral baths.

According to its brochure, Esalen was engaged in a radical exploration of "human potentiality." It was just beginning to receive media attention as a major source of the mind-blowing, erotic culture of the sixties. The Esalen authorites feared the media would be biased against them, on

< 2 >

the hunt for sensational stories about the baths and drugs and nudity and sex. I was urged, as a matter of fairness, to actively participate in program offerings, rather than to stay on the sidelines and observe. That seemed reasonable and I joined, with some misgivings, a five-day encounter workshop that offered "body movements, sensory awareness, fantasy experiments, psychodrama."

I had enrolled in a particularly aggressive group and from the beginning felt exposed and vulnerable. I decided on irony as the strategy for handling the new experience. The intense, intimate connection to strangers made the workshop seem to last for weeks, and toward the end, irony went out the window and I felt close to blowing up. The group leader saw that I was strung tight. He asked if I would be willing to take a fantasy trip. Where did he want to take me?

"Into your body to examine the stress you're under."

I said okay and at his instruction lay on the floor of the workshop room and closed my eyes. He asked me to imagine entering my body.

I imagined an enormous statue of myself, lying prone in a desert. I imagined my tiny self climbing into my open mouth and down my gullet and into my chest. I became absorbed by the effort and lost sense of the room and the group and heard only the leader's voice.

He asked, "Where are you?"

"In my chest."

"What do you see?"

"It's empty. There's nothing here."

"Where's your heart?

< 3 >

"There's no heart here."

He asked if I could bring a heart into my body and suddenly there it was, a pulsing heart sheathed in slimy membrane, the heart I'd imagined seeing twenty-three years before in the open chest of a dying German boy, and I broke down, wailing for a kid I thought I had long ago put out of mind. Other memories of war came up, equally vivid. The war, which had long been out of mind, was not yet finished.

The war years were perhaps the most dramatic of my life, responsible for habits of mind that shaped my generation. It is hard to distinguish events as they were and as they have become in memory. And yet when I recall the smell of a cup of hot coffee on an icy morning in Belgium more than fifty years ago it seems more real than the cup of tea I drank this morning.

The Medic is based on my experience as a combat medic. It takes its shape from a memoir published in the *New York Times Magazine* in May 1995. I have modified and dramatized the memoir, merging impressions—some vague, many vivid—of wartime encounters. I have invented names so that no one I served with would be confused by the composites of people, places, and units. The First Platoon, A Company, is itself a composite of units in which I served. The town I have called Grossdorf has a wartime model in Saxony but its geography has been altered to conform to my imagination since my memory here is vague. However, the city of Chemnitz will still be on the horizon. There will no longer be a camp containing Russian women slave laborers, but that camp was once

< 4 >

there, as was the camp of Hungarian Jewish women outside Kassel, Germany.

What I vouch for in this dramatized version of my service is the transforming intensity of war—the shellings, the entrenching, the wounded and dying, the Sauer crossing, marching fire, the sex, the loot, the Paris leave, Marishka, the encounter with the Russians, the war's end.

< 5 >

CHAPTER 1

< LEAVING >

I had finished my first year at the University of Michigan when my number came up. It was February 1943. The university was in a war mode, students in uniform, graduations accelerated, programs designed to serve the war effort. I wanted to be useful, too, and changed my major preference from literature to premed.

One morning in early March, my parents drove me to the Michigan Central Station in downtown Detroit, the jumping-off point for local draftees.

My father, at the time a greenhorn from Russia who spoke greenhorn English, had served in the First World War. He still had a martial bearing—a tough, muscular, little man who spoke with an accent.

He told me in his deep baritone, "When I left for war, I had no mama or papa to come with me to say good-bye."

"I could have come by myself," I said.

"That's not what I mean."

"Your pa means," my mother said, with the same slight accent as his, an intermingling of Yiddish and Russian, "that from the first he relied only on himself. He has become strong to serve his people and his family. You can always depend on him. He is always there for you. That's what he means to say."

She mediated between us as usual, softening his hard view of the world and easing my irritation.

"Your mother is more a politican than me," Dad said, "but she is right that whatever happens you must keep us informed. Do not spare us anything. Wherever you are, whatever happens, you should rely on us."

I looked around the station. There were thousands in my shoes. Twelve million were serving worldwide. I was part of it all and that was a thrill. I told them I'd be fine, not to worry.

If he had been able to pass on to me his toughness and fearlessness, he would have felt less anxiety as train whistles blew and engines began to churn and his naive, callow eighteen-year-old son prepared to join other soldier boys being hauled off to war.

When my group was summoned I pried myself from his embrace, received a last kiss from her.

"We love you, son."

Halfway down the ramp I looked back and waved and was on my way.

AT THE BATTLE CREEK induction center I was interviewed, tested, and assigned to a medical detachment in South Carolina. It was a disappointment. I didn't want to be in the medical corps. Medics carried no weapons. They operated under the rules of the Geneva Convention and

< 8 >

had the status of noncombatants. They were obliged to treat enemy wounded as well as their own. I had no desire to give aid to the enemy. I had imagined myself an armed, vengeful warrior. Still, giving aid was my assignment and I was resolved to do my best.

< 9 >

CHAPTER 2

< BAPTISM >

Each morning we sat baking in a red clay South Carolina field while officers and noncoms lectured us on first aid. We were told all that could happen, from blisters to amputations, and taught the proper responses. For blisters, draw the fluid, clean with Merthiolate, cushion with gauze. For amputations, apply a tourniquet, cover the stump, inject morphine to prevent shock. Get the patient in shock position and keep him warm.

I bought army manuals at the PX and studied the bones of the body and the major muscles and the circulation of blood and the techniques of bandaging and the venereal diseases from clap to lymphogranuloma inguinale. When the instructor's questions drew a blank from everyone else, I volunteered the answers.

I didn't realize I was off on the wrong foot, an eager-beaver college boy among southern farmers and working-class kids. Others in the detachment had driven ambulances or worked as hospital orderlies. Some of the least literate were expert at first aid. When I bandaged a GI simulating a broken clavicle, instead of a neat mummy, hand strapped to the chest, the upper torso swathed in two-inch gauze, there was a tangle of loose folds undone by the first movement.

"Ah, well," I said, "better luck next time."

Sergeant Carrol, unbinding my mannequin, then rewrapping it with flourishes of gauze, muttered, "How the hell did you get into this outfit?"

Dewey Carrol was tall and fat, his belt notched beneath a swollen paunch. Instead of lymphogranuloma inguinale he said "blue balls." He had deft fingers and a fumbling mouth. He knew the whole repertoire of bandaging and could wrap any part of a man. It didn't please him that I had the words he lacked and none of his skill. I stopped volunteering answers, but the damage was already done.

We practiced giving each other injections, angling the needle for the different shots—subcutaneous, intramuscular, intravenous. I didn't flinch when my novice buddy punctured my arm. When I jabbed in return I pierced a vein and stained his forearm with a bruise.

Dewey Carrol said, "With hands like that you got a tough job eating breakfast. Too bad you can't work with your mouth. Then you'd be champ."

I said, "Touché!" and spent the rest of the day grinding pots and pans with steel wool until the kitchen shut down.

In time I picked up the knack of bandaging, learned pressure points, how to give shots, all the business of first aid. I was good at drill, never fell out on marches, made good time over the obstacle course. But nothing I did

< 11 >

changed Dewey Carrol's first impression and his dislike spread to other noncoms.

A buck sergeant named Johnson came alongside while we were on a fifteen-mile march. It was a blazing day, the sun ferocious. I could see the heat working on him. He poured sweat and his freckled red skin looked boiled. He mirrored my step, said nothing for a few minutes, then, out of the blue, asked in a sly, innocent way, "Is it true, Leo, a Jew is just a nigger turned inside out?" He made it sound as if he were asking someone in a position to know a legitimate anatomical question. He stayed in step, at my hip, a beefy, ruddy man, with a plump, burning, freckled face, waiting for a response.

I had been taught never to use the word "nigger," and that if we were all turned inside out we'd find no differences, so, in a sense, I had to agree with Johnson. I should have said, The only thing I wouldn't want to be if I were turned inside out is you, Johnson. I said, "Too bad you're wearing those stripes."

"The nigger turned inside out thinks I shouldn't be wearing these stripes. Why don't you try taking them away?"

He may have been drinking. Maybe it was the sun. The challenge was crazy and I shut up. Harry Roman, a burly private from Polish Hamtramck, marching next to me, couldn't stomach the offense.

"Why don't you wear your stripes on your ass, where they'd fit better?"

That got laughs and Johnson scowled and dropped to the rear. Harry told me to ignore the bum. Johnson, he

< 12 >

said, had no life outside the army. "He sees someone like you who goes to college and who maybe thinks he's better than him and he'll try to screw you."

"I don't think I'm better than him."

"You are," Harry said. "Who isn't?"

THERE WAS ONE other collegian in our outfit, Joe Witty, also from the University of Michigan, a sophomore like me. He was tall and wellborn and generally favored. Joe Witty volunteered no answers. He offered his judgment only when asked and then he was authoritative. He was helped by a fine, deep voice whose tone was more convincing than any good argument. Joe Witty was a natural leader, aimed for Officer Candidate School after basic training. When he was invited to lead drill he was as good as any noncom. Anyone who lagged in preparing for inspection got reamed by Joe Witty. He didn't want screwups in any outfit he was connected with. Dewey Carrol recognized future brass and scraped low for Joe Witty.

I hoped that since we were both college boys from the University of Michigan, in the same sophomore class, the respect given him would rub off on me, but it didn't happen.

Witty was chosen to lead the current events discussion in our Information and Education class. The issue of the day was a coal miner's strike. Witty rallied us against the strikers. The goldbricks were striking for a larger share of the pie while we had to serve our country for a miserable sixty-five a month. He didn't put it exactly like that but that was the tenor. Witty came from the rich suburb of

< 13 >

Grosse Pointe outside Detroit. His father was a Detroit surgeon. I doubt that he'd ever have to complain about his working conditions.

I was on the other side of the political fence. My dad was a labor organizer, president of a truck drivers union. He was all for the coal miners and accused the mine owners of using the war effort as an excuse to weaken the union.

I spoke up against Joe Witty and talked about the hazards of coal mining—the fires, the cave-ins, the silicosis, the black lung. I said something like, The union is trying to guarantee miners a living wage and safe working conditions.

Joe Witty said, "What horseshit."

I said, "'Information and Education' isn't the same thing as propaganda."

Someone said, "Why don't you shut up," and that seemed to be the general feeling, and I shut up while Joe Witty kept talking.

I admired his physical grace and his confidence and his great voice and frat-boy good looks. I'd hoped we would hit it off, but he put me on the same list as unpatriotic striking miners, and I think most of the men agreed with him. They may have been working class, but they were suspicious of unions and suspicious of me.

That night I slid into bed and was brought up short by a doubled-over sheet. There were guffaws and snorts of laughter. I stood in the center of the barracks in my khaki GI underwear, a raging fool, and dared whoever was responsible to face me man to man. More guffaws. A skinny

< 14 >

kid named Lowry placed himself behind me and aped my outrage. I wheeled, grabbed him in a headlock, dragged him toward the latrine. Dewey Carrol came out from his room and pried us apart.

"Kill each other off the base. This is no damn playground."

Lowry screamed, "It wasn't me, you damn kike."

Later I saw his ears were red and bruised where I'd squeezed. I went up to him and apologized for losing control.

I said, "Don't ever again call me what you called me."

He nodded glumly, still humiliated.

I asked Harry Roman, "Why do I let myself get sucked into something so stupid?"

"You should be pissed off. They made a fool of you. Me, I'd kill."

Harry was nineteen, a few months older than me, a big-shouldered, brown-haired, blue-eyed Pole. In Detroit he hung out at the Paradise and other black-and-tan show clubs. He was crazy about Count Basie and Duke Ellington and Billie Holiday and didn't moderate his opinions though we were in a Jim Crow army in the Jim Crow South. In Columbia Negroes stepped off sidewalks into the street when a white man approached, and "nigger lover" was as virulent a curse as a man could make. Harry liked what he liked, said what he wanted to say, and—as far as he could get away with it—did what he wanted to do.

We went together on a pass to Columbia. There were no bars or liquor stores in town—South Carolina was a dry state. Harry introduced me to bootleg whiskey. I took one

< 15 >

throat-clenching swig from an unlabeled bottle and that was enough. I was probably too tame for Harry. We liked each other, traveled together for a time, then drifted apart.

I KNEW WITTY disliked me. In the barracks he gave me the cold shoulder. I said, "Hello, Joe," and he shrugged. When we met in town he greeted everyone in our group but refused to look at me. I asked Harry, "Am I right? Does he mean to insult me?"

Harry said, "The guy doesn't like you."

"It's stupid, a kid's game."

Harry said, "Forget it. He's an asshole."

I tried to accept Witty's dislike as a fact of barracks life but it hurt when he erased me, and one day he went too far, and I was humiliated. We had just finished a speed march, nine miles in two hours, up a dusty road, a hundred degrees, every man lobster red, first striding in cadence, then jogging, beginning to gasp early in the game, wobbling under the burden of full packs, trailed by an ambulance that inched up on stragglers and accumulated the fallen. Afterward we lined up naked in the latrine, waiting to get into the shower room, yelling to those already showering to hurry it up. Witty was in the shower and heard only my voice.

"Step in here and I'll kick the shit out of you."

I couldn't believe he was serious and stepped into the shower with all the showers going. He pushed me and I stumbled along duckboards. He pressed me against the wall, cocked his fist, almost hit, then shoved me away.

"Why get in trouble over you?"

< 16 >

I soaked for a minute, then followed him into the latrine where he was toweling off. "Let's go back of the barracks."

"I'm not getting in trouble over you." He put a stress of contempt into the "you." "If you want to fight, meet me in the gym, with gloves."

I was bowled over by his dislike. If we'd have gone in back of the barracks I could only have pawed him.

I said, "In the gym, then," unable to keep my voice steady. "Whenever you want."

He was leaving for Charleston on a three-day pass. When he got back he was headed for surgical technician training. He would return in two weeks. "Two weeks from Monday, before retreat, we'll meet in the gym. That satisfy you?" It was said easily, as if he were transacting ordinary business, but there was the same stress of contempt when he said "you."

"Two weeks from Monday. I'll be there."

I was ashamed and didn't tell Harry what had happened in the shower room. I didn't want to lose his respect. I went instead to a friend in Headquarters Company.

I had met Jason Diedrich in the music room of the post USO. He was a Harvard undergraduate, majoring in classics. He introduced me to his three Harvard buddies, also with Headquarters. The four of them had a room of their own in the Headquarters barracks.

Jason was very bright. He made sense of everything. I wanted him to make sense of my encounter with Joe Witty. I told him I'd stood there as if I couldn't be insulted. I'd been humiliated.

< 17 >

It was a battle, he said, that I couldn't win. "Get out of it, Leo."

Jason had a monkish appearance, a narrow, severe face perched on a long throat, a wide thin mouth. He wore plain GI spectacles. His model was a Frère Lupus Servatus who preserved Ovid despite a shortage of parchment for more pious work. Servatus faked allegiance to his superiors in order to save what he loved, and Jason said that was also his intention. During the working day he was a Head-quarters clerk. After hours he attended to the Greeks and Romans.

I asked Jason how I could get out of it.

He had pull and Headquarters needed another clerk. If I was interested he'd see about getting me transferred.

I had dreamed of combat, and dropping out would have left me weak and defeated. I said, "No, thanks," to Jason.

Harry Roman came up with a better proposal. The air force needed pilots and navigators and bombardiers and advertised a training program for qualified infantry per-sonnel. Why not apply for a transfer to the air force?

I said, "Absolutely!"

We met with First Sergeant Murphy, a career army man. Harry told him we wanted to apply for the air force program.

"What makes you think you're qualified?"

"That's what we want to find out."

"I hear you're a couple of fuckups."

Harry said, "Then you're better off without us, Sarge."

Murphy reached to the shelves behind his desk and brought out blank forms.

< 18 >

"Fill these out and get them back to me. Nothing's going to happen till you finish basic training and that's no sure thing for you smart-asses."

I HOPED WHEN Witty returned he would see our differences as stupid—unworthy of someone headed for OCS—and call off the fight. After two weeks he showed up in the barracks in his tie and overseas cap and summer tans. He was among a crowd of buddies gathered around his bed and footlocker. He spotted me at my end of the barracks. He shouted genially—no one would have guessed what he was proposing—"Next Monday, before retreat."

The prospect of the fight had preoccupied me for two weeks. It didn't seem to have troubled him at all.

IT WAS THE WORST possible time for my mother to choose to visit. She wrote that they were disturbed by my letters. I had revealed nothing, but the tone seemed depressed. They feared something was wrong and she was delegated to find out since Dad was tied up with strike preparations and couldn't come himself. She already had a railroad ticket and a hotel reservation. She would arrive on Friday morning and stay till Monday. She wrote, "I do not expect you to meet me at the station. I will wait for you in the hotel."

The last thing I wanted was for her to visit. I called home, caught her as she was about to leave, told her flatly not to come, that this was the worst possible time.

"Are you in trouble?"

< 19 >

I was too busy. We were going out in the field. There would be weeklong bivouacs. I didn't know whether I could get passes to Columbia. Anyhow, basic training was over and I'd soon be home on furlough. It was crazy for her to suffer a miserable two-day trip in a crowded train.

She'd see me whenever I was available.

"Please, Mom, don't come."

"I'll see you on Friday."

I considered going to Witty and telling him my family was coming and that I'd have to delay the fight, but it would have been too shameful.

I took his measure across the barracks. He was several inches taller, not as broad across the chest and shoulders, probably the same weight, and with an air of confidence I lacked. I didn't want to fight him.

Fort Jackson, with thirty thousand GIs, had overwhelmed the city of Columbia. Columbia still had charming neighborhoods but the main street had been reduced to honky-tonk quality. Schlock shops peddled army insignia and identification bracelets and uniform upgrades. The hotels were old and seedy. The two or three movie houses offered war films almost exclusively. Groups of horny GIs followed unaccompanied women, and I feared my petite, friendly mom would be harassed.

I met her after retreat. We talked about my training and Dad's approaching strike. She said he was developing a strike fund, organizing a picket line, responding to flyers that the bosses had sent to union brothers pleading with them not to strike; that a strike would jeopardize the war effort. Dad answered with his flyers. He reminded them

< 20 >

that he had raised thousands of dollars for war bonds and had a son in the army and would do anything in his power to defeat Hitler. In boldface at the end of the flyer, Do not be misled. Fight to preserve your rights.

Our conversations were strained and edgy. She knew I was hiding something, and when she probed, I came close to exploding.

We ate junk food; there was no other kind. We suffered through a John Wayne movie that seemed pointless and untrue.

I apologized for not spending more time with her.

She said, "It's enough being with you even for a little while."

I felt guilty about leaving her alone in town. I didn't know how she would get along when I wasn't around.

"My dear boy, most of my life you weren't around and yet somehow I managed. I am not a frail person."

We sat in the small lounge of the hotel on her last evening, jammed together on a mildewed sofa. It was the day before I was to meet Joe Witty in the gym.

She said, "I speak to the soldiers on the street. They are nice boys."

I told her she was too trusting. "You have no sense of danger. This isn't your hometown, remember."

"My hometown was Zhitomir. In Zhitomir I had good reason to be careful. I learned very early to have a sense of danger. Columbia, South Carolina, is not Zhitomir. Did I ever tell you about how I went to school when I was nine years old? It's maybe a story I haven't told you."

There was a quota on Jewish schoolchildren and she

< 21 >

couldn't get into elementary school until she was nine years old. Her father, an estate manager, used his influence and she finally was allowed into a parochial school. Each morning she walked along a river path that took her through a peasant neighborhood. The men sat on their porch steps and when she passed shouted, "Little kike, where do you think you're going?" They cursed her parents and all the other Jews of Zhitomir. When she started hurrying they turned their dogs loose. Each morning she was hounded into the river and arrived at school drenched. It happened for almost three weeks. She didn't tell her father. She feared he would pull her out of school. Her teachers asked how come she was soaked. She refused to say and they threatened to suspend her but she pleaded, and since she was the best student in class, they let her stay, warning her to behave properly. She started earlier in the morning, before the peasants were out, and finally her tormentors lost interest and she was able to pass through their neighborhood without incident.

"We knew these people," she said. "They lived hard lives. Drunk, they were terrible. Sober, they were altogether different. The same ones who cursed me and turned their dogs on me later invited me into their homes for tea. Someone put them up to being so cruel."

I asked who put them up to it and she told me thugs called the Black Hundreds, enlisted by the czar to persecute Jews. My father, she said, had fought the Black Hundreds.

She knew his life as if it were a legend. I'd heard her tell his story often. He started as a pious boy, aimed for the

< 22 >

rabbinate. When the Black Hundreds came to Zhitomir and afflicted the Jews, his faith was useless as a guide to action. The pious huddled like sheep, waiting to be slaughtered and it wasn't in him to be a sheep. He threw off his faith, renounced the Bible as a fairy-tale account of origins, and took on as a more practical guide to action a man from Lithuania he knew only as Josef who brought weapons to the Zhitomir Jews and led recruits into the woods and taught them to shoot.

My dad was fourteen years old when he joined skirmishes against the Black Hundreds. He fought for two years. One night a dozen police came to his home, searched it, found his *kinzov*—a double-edged blade—evidence enough to charge him with revolutionary activity.

He was jailed first in Zhitomir, then sent to a prison in Kiev, and from there to a prison in Moscow. He was transported by train with other convicts to Yarensk on the edge of Siberia. He was exiled for a year, the sentence perhaps mitigated because he was only sixteen years old.

My mother had watched as they marched him in chains to the Zhitomir jail. She was eight years old and stood curbside with her mother and father as the political prisoners were hauled away.

She knew I had problems. She could see how tense and unhappy I was. "We are strong people," she said. "We stand together. We have overcome great troubles."

I told her I had problems, who didn't, but nothing I couldn't handle.

"Fine," she said. "I am relieved." She told me how strong and handsome I looked. She was confident I would

< 23 >

overcome my troubles just as she and my father had. She said, "I love you, my boy," and I said, "I love you, Mom." I almost told her what I faced the next day with Joe Witty, but it could only have made her miserable. We said good-bye that night. I didn't tell anyone she was visiting. Every-one in my outfit belonged to a different world and would fall out of my life. She would always be with me.

I was miserable during her visit. I couldn't release my-self from the date with Witty. I couldn't stop the scenarios of defeat and humiliation rolling through my mind.

On my way back to the base after our last visit, I missed her intensely.

WHEN A MAN'S in shock, his face is gray, he's in a cold sweat, his pulse is fluttery. The blood leaves the brain and collects in the solar plexus and elsewhere. Blood ves-sels collapse. The brain brooks no starving and will perish from the insult. Lift the legs, lower the head. Give plasma to raise the pressure in the veins.

There was cold sweat on my face, blood in my belly. The gym was a great shed with naked steel beams, sun dazzling through clerestories. We were beneath an ele-vated running track. In an opposite corner were mats for wrestlers and tumblers. Basketball games occupied the center of the gym. Balls pounded, shoes thudded, players called for passes. I heard rims vibrate from missed shots.

We faced each other in our corner of the gym, wearing sixteen-ounce gloves, stripped down to GI shorts. Once it started fear was gone. We circled each other. I launched punches. He jabbed. Wild swings. We clinched, pounded

< 24 >

backs. This went on for several minutes, neither of us much hurt, both of us breathing hard, holding on in clinches. Just before the whistle that summoned us to retreat, he hit me in the eye with the lacings of his glove and I swung with purpose, but couldn't hurt him. The fight ended in a clinch.

"Okay," Witty gasped, "it's time."

I was shaking and exhilarated.

We walked to the locker room without speaking. I looked in the mirror and saw that I had a bruised eye.

"It's not enough."

"Time for retreat," he said.

NO MORE SHORT-SHEETING, no more disrespect. No one troubled me or Harry. We were destined for the air force and were already considered gone. I continued with advanced medical training while waiting for the transfer. We marched into the countryside for war games. I did stints at the division hospital.

I was sent out on rifle-range duty. It was early fall, still hot weather. The rifle range was a lazy job for a medic. I wore full combat gear—red cross brassards pinned to each shoulder, steel helmet marked with red crosses on a white field, two medical kits suspended from a shoulder harness, anchored by a pistol belt. My kits held gauze bandages, ammonia capsules, small compresses, belly compresses, aspirin, bismuth and paregoric, bandage scissors, tape, Merthiolate, sulfa packets, sodium Amytal tablets, a hypodermic needle for blisters, tags for the wounded, and morphine Syrettes for shock.

I took off my kits, lay under a tree, took it easy while GIs fired at targets.

Behind us was Battle Village, dotted with minefields, strung with barbed wire. GIs wiggled beneath the wire. Machine guns fired overhead. Dynamite blasts simulated artillery. Infantrymen charged the mocked-up village and shot at targets in windows. Bazooka teams aimed at immobilized tanks.

With these cozy sounds of battle as background, I sent my dreams ahead to scout the terrain of war. I dreamed of what could happen if someone shouted, Aid Man! I'd hook up my pistol belt, run toward the wounded soldier, my hands on my kits to keep them from flapping. Once I reached him, then what? What if it was a chest wound, the cavity penetrated? I'd been instructed to use anything at hand to plug the hole and keep the lungs from collapsing. What if an artery was severed? A tourniquet tied too long meant gangrene. Each move I made risked a man's life. This wasn't where I wanted to be. I didn't want to give aid. I had no particular calling as a medic. Better to enter combat as a warrior with no obligation to help anyone.

I was almost asleep, thinking about Joe Witty— reduced to ordinary size, no longer the villain of my fantasy. I had a clearer view of his strength and weakness, was a fool to have overestimated him.

I heard someone yell, "Aid Man!" Then again, *"Aid Man!"* I was half-asleep and dreamy and had imagined just this wail. *"Aid Man!"* I turned on an elbow and looked toward Battle Village. The dynamite blasts had stopped. The machine guns had stopped. There was no sound of fir-

< 26 >

ing anywhere. A GI ran across the field waving wildly. I recognized a trim platoon sergeant from C Company, one of the permanent cadre who had been to Ranger school and could jog fifteen miles with a full pack and not show the strain. *"Aid Man!"* Raging, as though I'd done something terrible. He ran up to me. He shouted in my face, *"Aid Man!"* He grabbed my shoulders, his mouth agape, heaving air.

"A man got his leg blowed off. Let's go."

I woke up the ambulance driver. I secured my kits. The three of us jumped into the ambulance. We slammed across the field toward Battle Village.

A squad leader had tripped into a hole just as a dynamite charge exploded. "His leg's off," the sergeant said. "His foot's still in the shoe."

The ambulance launched in the air, slammed down on the field, the carriage groaning. The ambulance driver hit every furrow. We bounced high, my kits slamming my thighs.

A group of GIs were clustered at a shell hole. A lieutenant crouched over a man covered by a blanket. They stepped aside for me. I saw a shoe a few yards away. I pulled back the blanket and looked. Gone at the calf, the flesh shredded. A hot, shitty smell, the skin peppered, a tourniquet tied above the knee. I untied the tourniquet; blood spurted onto the blanket. I could see the torn flesh, gristle, the artery gulping, the veins pinched shut. I retied the tourniquet, the flow of blood reduced to a slow welling. The scissors came out and I cut away the pant leg. The Syrette came out. I thrust the plunger into the hollow nee-

< 27 >

dle and broke the seal. I jammed the needle into his thigh and squeezed it out like toothpaste. I could feel muscles jumping. My hand was slimy where I touched the blanket.

We lifted him onto a stretcher and into the ambulance.

The ambulance driver went fast. I braced against the cab sides while trying to figure out how to bandage the stump. I raised his leg to get a bandage roll underneath and he reared and screamed. I yelled at the driver to slow down.

I took out a large compress and placed it over the stump and looped the strings around the upper calf.

He screamed, "My balls!"

I opened his pants, looked at his balls. Darts of powder peppered the sac and the surrounding flesh.

I told him, "You're okay."

They were waiting for us at the post hospital with a stretcher on wheels. Four orderlies carried him from the ambulance. A white-smocked doctor lifted the belly compress as they wheeled him toward emergency.

I called after them, "I gave him morphine. An eighth of a grain." They were already inside when I remembered that I had forgotten to fill out the tag. Describe the wound, its treatment, give your name, rank, serial number, and medical organization.

The ambulance driver said, "You did great."

We returned to the rifle range but the day was finished.

They had heard back at the detachment. The lieutenant who tied the tourniquet had called to praise me.

Our CO, a southern doctor, slapped my back. "Nice going, son."

I'd made him scream in the ambulance. The belly com-

< 28 >

press hadn't been neatly tied. I'd looped the free strings over his leg and fumbled with the knot. A clumsy job. But good enough for Joe Witty.

"Listen," he said, "whatever we've had going let's call it off." His hand reached for mine; we shook hands. "You did great out there." He was boyish and charming. "I hear the leg was off. Entirely off. Nice going, buddy." He tapped my arm with his fist.

My bloody field jacket was good enough credentials for Joe Witty. He invited me to the PX for a beer after retreat. There he advertised me as a credit to our outfit. "This is the medic who handled that amputation on the rifle range to-day." He went on to speak of campus life as if we owned a common experience.

He was a kid like me, foolish like me. That knowledge both connected us and released us.

The air force application was approved. Harry and I transferred to Miami Beach. I went on to school in Sioux City, Iowa; he went elsewhere. Two months into the air force training, the war in Europe took a turn for the worse; there was a demand for infantry, and the program was terminated. I was sent to an infantry division, again a medic, this time an aid man attached to a rifle platoon. I went on bivouacs and field maneuvers with my new unit. We trained through the spring and fall of 1944. In late fall we bobbed and rocked on a Liberty Ship in Boston Harbor. We joined a long convoy and crossed the North Atlantic in rough seas on our way to England. We idled in Bournemouth until early winter and then embarked across the channel for the ruined port of Le Havre. We crammed

< 29 >

into boxcars outside Le Havre. It was already freezing. We dismounted in northern France, snow on the ground. We immediately dug in. We were warned to be on guard. Germans, dressed as GIs, speaking vernacular English, had infiltrated our lines. We were warned not to move out of the company area without knowing the password. We dug our first trenches in frozen ground. We experienced our first shelling. My first battlefield death was a GI whose trench collapsed after a shell hit close. We dug him out. I put him on his belly, turned his face to the side, cleared his mouth and throat, straddled him, hands on his ribs, and pressed down in rhythm with my own breathing, the old method of artificial respiration. I worked until I was too exhausted to care but couldn't bring him to life.

It was easy to become a veteran. You only needed to survive. A few more casualties and I was promoted to Technician Fifth Grade, the rank of corporal.

I HAD FOLLOWED my dreams into combat. There I met the dead and dying and faced my own death. It was all I wanted when I first dreamed of war.

< 30 >

CHAPTER 3

< BELGIAN WINTER, 1945 >

That winter the Germans were in full retreat on all fronts. In the west the Allies had reached the German border. In the east the German invasion of Russia had been reversed and the Russians were aiming for Berlin and closing fast.

My regiment was in Luxembourg about to cross into Germany at the Sauer River. It wouldn't be an easy crossing. The bridge was down at Echternach. The east bank of the river rose sharply. The Germans had mined roads and trails on the other side; artillery zeroed in on crossing points. The rumor circulated that General Patton, directing the operation as head of the Third Army, meant to force his way into Germany even at the cost of a truckload of dog tags collected from dead GIs.

My company was spared. We remained in reserve on the Belgium-Luxembourg side of the Sauer, preparing withdrawal positions in case the assault failed and the Germans counterattacked.

We dug slit trenches up and down a hillside a few kilometers from the river. We dug every day until the light gave out. We scraped away snow, swung picks at the frozen ground, shoved quarter-pound sticks of dynamite a foot down, lit the fuse, and got out of the way. Afterward we cleared out slit trenches, four feet deep, two to three feet wide, six feet long. We axed saplings and tree limbs, crossed them over the trench, leaving an opening in back to squeeze through, another in front for a field of vision. We covered the roof with soil, then camouflaged the works with snow.

Winter's ferocity was unexpected. We had no special winter issue. A single wool blanket barely cut the freeze. At night we lay in trenches, huddling against each other for body heat, belly against rump.

I was the first platoon medic and at morning sick call I began to see cases of flu. My instructions were to keep them up front. If the fever didn't rage it wasn't hot enough; if the wound didn't kill or incapacitate it wasn't serious enough; if someone begged to go back to battalion he wasn't crazy enough. A man might say, I'm dying, and I'd give him aspirin for the pain. If he had diarrhea I dispensed bismuth and paregoric.

I heard of cases of trench foot—toes blackened, skin dead white, a putrid smell coming from spongy flesh. Gangrene and amputation followed if circulation wasn't restored. The prevention was to keep feet dry. Every night we paired off and rubbed each other's feet and put on dry socks.

BILLY BAKER DIDN'T have anyone to rub his feet. He slept alone in a slit trench. Sergeant Lucca told him to pair up with someone.

< 32 >

"I can't find no one," Billy said.

The sergeant asked Rebel to dig in with Billy but Rebel said he and Alfieri were already a pair. The sergeant went to Stanky who shared a trench with Fisher and Coleman.

"One of you has to dig in with Billy Baker."

Stanky said he'd rather take company punishment. Fisher and Coleman felt the same way.

No one wanted to dig in with Billy, a notorious bed wetter. He had somehow managed to hide the fact when he got into the army, but once assigned to our platoon barracks his shame was discovered and he was afterward shunned as dim-witted and unclean.

Sergeant Lucca asked if I could get Billy reassigned for medical reasons. "If he can't control his piss what's he going to hit with his M-one? He's more a threat to us than to the krauts. Let's send him back where he can't do any damage."

I asked Billy if he'd like to be transferred to a rear unit where he'd have hot meals and be warm and safe. Maybe he'd even be sent back to the States, a deal any frontline GI would sacrifice arms or legs to get.

Billy didn't want to go back. "I do my best," he said. "It happens less and less."

"He's found a home," I told the sergeant. "He won't leave."

It ended with Billy digging in with me and Sergeant Lucca. At night we rubbed his feet and made sure he put on dry socks and warned him not to piss.

• • •

< 33 >

HE HAD LITTLE to say about himself. He was a farm boy from Alabama.

"What kind of farm?"

He shrugged.

"Were there tractors? Combines?"

He said a Model A Ford pickup and two mules.

"Cows, chickens?"

"One cow," he said. "Pigs. Chickens."

Lucca told me it was no use trying to draw him out. Billy wasn't eager to remember a scruffy Alabama farm that even pigs and chickens didn't favor. "This slit trench is probably the closest that lonesome son of a bitch has ever come to having a home."

ONE MORNING BILLY reported to sick call with a black and swollen thumb. He told me he didn't want to complain but he was having a hard time digging.

I asked Captain Roth if there was room in the company jeep to take Billy to the aid station.

"Is it an emergency?"

"It's not life or death. He's got a bad thumb."

"Wait till the jeep goes to battalion so we don't have to make a special trip."

I bandaged Billy's thumb and excused him from digging. Later that day the jeep took him to Battalion Aid. I didn't know how he had been treated until the next morning when the captain came to our platoon and called me over. "Private Baker is going to lose his thumb, Corporal. If you'd have told me how serious it was we could have gotten him back in time."

< 34 >

I told him I was just a T-5 aid man, not a doctor.

"You don't have to be a goddamn doctor to have some common sense."

Billy returned from the aid station a day later, his thumb splinted and bandaged.

"It's okay," he said. "They told me I shouldn't dig."

I knew they'd never get his thumb; he never willingly let go of anything, including his piss, which left of its own will, not his. When the captain came around I said to him, "Private Baker is here and so is his thumb, sir."

He shrugged. "You're lucky this time, Corporal."

CAPTAIN ROTH HAD needled me before but this time he got to me. I told Lucca I didn't have to take any shit from the captain. I could get reassigned to any company in the battalion. Everyone knew my reputation. They'd all be glad to have me. The platoon might end up with an aid man like the third platoon's Grace.

Lucca didn't want an aid man like Grace. "You're our man, Leo. Don't worry about the captain. If he gives you any trouble, come to me. I'll take care of him."

Sergeant Lucca was no burly, bass growler of a sergeant. He was a motherly man, slim, careful, thoughtful. When he said, "I'll take care of him," I understood him to mean he would take care of the captain as he took care of the platoon, keeping everything sane and orderly and reasonable.

THIS IS WHAT Sergeant Lucca didn't like about Grace, the third platoon aid man. A few weeks before, we

< 35 >

were probing the high ground near some Belgian village, and a Third Platoon scout was hit by a sniper. He lay in the road up ahead, facedown, on his belly. The company took cover in the woods off the road. Aid man Grace crept to where he could see the scout lying in the road. "He's not moving. You can see he's dead. There's a sniper waiting to knock off anyone who goes out there."

Grace wouldn't go to him.

They called on Cooper, aid man with the Second Platoon. Cooper said the Third Platoon was Grace's responsibility, not his, and he wouldn't go to the scout either.

Sergeant Lucca came to me. "The Third Platoon has a man down out there and Grace and Cooper won't go."

I took off down the road, full speed, came up over the rise, saw the scout lying in the road, hit the ground next to him, turned him over, saw a nickel-sized wound on his forehead. I couldn't feel a pulse. I put my cheek to his mouth and there was no breath. I expected to be hit the same way, above the eyes, in the middle of the forehead. Either the sniper respected my red cross markings or he'd taken off.

Sergeant Lucca didn't want anything to do with an aid man like Grace. He wanted someone who would come for him if he was hit. "You're our man, Leo, not Grace."

Did he claim me for his own? That suited me fine.

LUCCA WASN'T THE only one to hear my complaint about Captain Roth. Cooper, another of the Alabamans in our outfit, told me to pay no mind to the JB.

"What's a JB?"

< 36 >

"A Jew Bastard."

Lucca said, "Roth's no Jew. He leads us to mass."

"He looks like an MOT," Cooper said.

I asked Cooper what an MOT was.

"Member of the Tribe."

"What do you mean he looks like an MOT?"

"You know. The nose and the big mouth."

"The captain's no Jew," Lucca said again.

"He might as well be," said Cooper.

Later I asked Lucca if Cooper knew I was a Jew.

"What does that redneck know besides rednecks? Don't worry about the captain, Leo. I'll keep him in line."

Cooper remained my friend. It didn't matter to him when I told him I was a Jew. I bullied him and cursed him but couldn't alter his map of the world where the Jews he didn't know were located at the outermost boundary among serpents and dragons.

THIS IS WHAT Sergeant Lucca had on Captain Roth. When the division was in England, waiting to cross the Channel, our company occupied a small seaside hotel in Bournemouth. It was the time of air raids and buzz bombs and there was a strict curfew. Captain Roth conducted bed check himself. He went through the hotel around ten at night. Lucca then shared a room with PFC Van Pelt, a nineteen-year-old classic Dutch boy: blond hair, red cheeks, juicy lips. Van Pelt was the company messenger at the time, though he later lost the job.

One night the captain sent Lucca to battalion headquarters for a briefing. Van Pelt was almost asleep when the

< 37 >

captain came by for bed check. The captain lingered by the bed, touched Van Pelt's throat. Van Pelt wasn't sure what the touch meant and pretended to be asleep. The captain, a dapper, by-the-book West Pointer, didn't seem a fatherly type.

A few nights later, with Lucca again at battalion, the captain put his hand under Van Pelt's covers. This time Van Pelt told Lucca what was happening. During the next bed check Lucca hid in the closet and caught Roth going under the covers.

"Can I speak to you in the hallway, sir?" The captain followed Lucca into the hallway.

"I think someone else should do bed check."

The captain nodded. "I'll see to it."

Lucca didn't mean to take it any further. Roth was a devout Catholic with a wife and kid. What happened had been an accident. Lucca was positive it wouldn't happen again. Anyway, he now had clout.

"If he gives you any trouble, Leo, I'll take care of it."

THE REST OF the battalion bridged the Sauer River at Echternach and climbed the high ridge into Germany. We could hear artillery operating nonstop at the front, a muffled boom, boom, boom, day and night. The battalion was being mauled at the Siegfried line across the river. At night the horizon pulsed with white-green light. Convoys of trucks and ambulances returned through our position. I pulled back the rear flap of a graves detail truck in a convoy stopped near our command and saw layers of dead GIs stacked like cordwood.

We'd soon have our turn on the other side of the Sauer.

< 38 >

Pillboxes and tank traps and barbed wire and minefields and artillery and machine guns waited for us.

While we were stalled there in Belgium we made our slit trenches as much like home as we could. We plastered the bottom with pine needles, covered the needles with our ponchos. Lucca borrowed a Coleman lantern from the cook and hung it from our roof, shaded with a GI towel. We joined our blankets together and lay there with our boots off, feet rubbed and wearing dry wool socks, wool caps pulled over our ears, listening to the distant boom-boom from Germany across the Sauer. It was the only home any of us—not only Billy Baker—believed in.

Someone found an old treadle sewing machine in the wreck of a house. It was still in working condition. Lucca's father was a tailor and Lucca knew the trade. He set up the sewing machine on the snow-filled road. He borrowed my bandage scissors and cut a pattern from the army newspaper. He sat on a wobbly, broken chair, pumping the treadle, and made face hoods out of GI blankets. He outfitted the entire platoon.

THE PROCEDURE WE were given for taking a pillbox was this. The artillery laid down a rolling barrage of smoke and shells. Engineers crawled behind the barrage to clear a path through the minefield. They were followed by men who set long pipes of explosive under coils of barbed wire. That opened the way for someone to crawl to the pillbox and place a butterfly charge against the concrete wall. Once the pillbox was torn open a flamethrower scoured the inside and we moved in.

< 39 >

The strategy rarely worked smoothly. Tracer fire lit up the hills from another tier of pillboxes. Artillery was zeroed in. The assault sometimes didn't get past the wire. The butterfly man, under a bulky pack, was an easy target. If his pack was hit only shards of him would be recovered.

Lucca asked for volunteers for a platoon assault team. He needed someone to carry the explosive. Billy Baker said, "I will." He was an ideal butterfly man, too dim to anticipate dying. Lucca told him it was a simple job. All he had to do was place the pack with the shaped charge against the wall of the pillbox, trigger the fuse, then crawl away as fast as he could. He told Billy it was the most important job in the assault. Billy was glad to be our butterfly man and didn't need convincing.

"Ask him to take the Siegfried line," I told Lucca, "and he won't stop until he gives you Berlin."

Billy adored Sergeant Lucca, and who didn't? When I risked sniper fire to reach the wounded scout I was no braver than Grace or Cooper, who had refused to go out there. I was numb and terrified. I had less of a sense of my needs than either of them. I did what I had no heart to do because I was ready to die for Lucca's good word. He told me what to wear, what to eat, how to survive. I sometimes didn't have the foggiest idea where we were until Lucca told me, and then I felt located.

I didn't share his sympathy for Captain Roth. It wasn't until I suffered my own loss of confidence that I understood what Lucca knew all along, that Roth wasn't suited to command, that it was torture for Roth to keep up appearances. He may have looked the part—held tight,

< 40 >

braced like a West Point cadet—but he was split by the strain. Lucca tried to keep him intact. It was a vain kindness.

Sergeant Lucca should have been our commanding officer.

MAURICE SULLY CAME to me one night, after we had quit digging.

"I hear you speak French."

"Not much. Just high school French."

"Good enough."

"Good enough for what?"

"We can do better than C rations, Doc."

The next evening after digging he asked me to come with him and his buddy Nagy to forage the countryside. We might find fresh eggs, meat, wine. Who knows? Maybe even mademoiselles.

Nagy asked Maurice, "You going to eat them, too, the mademoiselles?"

"No better source of protein," Maurice said.

The stumpy, muscle-bound Nagy was always at Maurice's heels. You could ask, "Walking your dog, Maurice?" and Nagy wouldn't take offense. He even seemed pleased. We asked, "Fed your animal lately, Maurice?" and Nagy got a giggle out of that.

The giggle about feeding had to do with an incident when Maurice Sully first joined us in Camp McCoy, Wisconsin, just before the division broke camp and went overseas. He was assigned the cot next to mine, a lean, weathered man with red hair, a trim ruddy mustache, a

< 41 >

sharp, foxy face. When he smiled he bared his teeth. He was older than we were, in his late twenties. Maurice had enlisted to escape trouble but he'd found more trouble instead. You could see the evidence on the arm of his fatigue shirt where there was the ghost of staff sergeant stripes. He had spent time in the stockade and been reduced to one of us.

When he first came into the barracks he saw the medical kits on my foot locker. "Got something for what ails me, Doc?"

"I can handle blisters, amputations, clap, stuff like that."

"What's in your bag for amputations?"

"Tourniquets to stop the bleeding, morphine to kill the pain."

"I'll take morphine. I got pain to kill."

I treated the request as a joke but afterward kept a close eye on my kits.

Maurice said he'd been in show business. To prove it he sang, did magic tricks. He pulled a pencil from his nose, shoved coins up his ears, did elaborate shuffles with a deck of cards. After a few PX beers he sang in a surprising tenor, a contrast to his hoarse, cigarette-eroded speaking voice, a song that finished with tenderness. Sleep tight, sweet children, time to hit the road.

A simple, sweet lyric from a man who wasn't sweet and certainly wasn't simple.

"I am an explorer of life," he once said to me. "I go to the border, say 'Fuck you' to no-trespassing signs, and cross over. Who knows what they're trying to keep from me?"

< 42 >

This is how Nagy came to be Maurice's dog. At first Nagy hated Maurice. His boundaries were sharp and Maurice baited him to the edge to watch him teeter. Nagy's rage and inarticulateness made him seem comic. His large-featured face disguised nothing. He was a terrible poker player who never learned from his losses. He was a perfect mark for any trickster willing to risk his fury. You could watch the progress of his thinking—a dim awareness, an increasing recognition, then a blowup when he realized he was the butt of a joke. Provoking him was one of Maurice's entertainments.

During our last days in Wisconsin we went on maneuvers deep into pine woods. We hiked fifteen miles with full packs to reach our bivouac area. The kitchen wasn't yet set up and we were hungry. There was a pond nearby; we stripped and went in. Someone caught a frog and started tossing it around. It reached Maurice and he said, "I'm hungry as hell," opened his mouth, and pressed his teeth down on the frog.

Stanky said he'd pay a buck to see Maurice bite all the way through.

"Okay," Maurice said, "but I need a couple slices of bread."

Someone went for bread.

Maurice said, "I use ketchup on my seafood." Someone got a dab of ketchup from the kitchen. By this time he had the whole platoon as audience. He told Hamilton to hold the palm-sized frog while he smeared ketchup on the bread. He put the frog between slices of bread, squeezing tight.

< 43 >

"You going to eat it like that, alive?" Nagy asked.

"Maybe I should kill it first. Naw," he said. "For five bucks more I'll eat it alive like the Hunky asked me."

"I didn't ask you!" Nagy shouted.

Hamilton offered a buck. Fisher and Stanky said they'd make up the rest.

Sergeant Lucca, coming from company headquarters, asked what was happening.

"Maurice is having some live seafood."

Lucca said, "Gimme that." He pulled the frog sandwich from Maurice and let the frog spring free.

"I would have ate it."

"Not while I'm around," Lucca said.

A few days later we saw a movie at the post theater with Rita Hayworth. Back in barracks Maurice said, "Ooh, I could dig up there with a spoon it looks so tasty."

Nagy asked, "You'd eat that?"

"Rita? Any day, Hunky."

It was a time when no working-class man spoke of oral sex save with repugnance or as a joke, and Maurice didn't seem to be joking. Nagy, a burly stump, with a Neanderthal head, a truck driver in civilian life, asked, "You got no disgust?"

"Don't tell me you only eat what they tell you to eat. No mind of your own, Hunky?"

Nagy said, "I ought to take you out in back of the barracks and kick the shit out of you."

That night, lights out, we heard a panicked Nagy shout, "What you doing on my bed?"

Nagy's bed exploded. They crashed on the floor and

< 44 >

struggled. Then Nagy said, in a strangled voice, "Let go." After a moment's silence he said, "You're a strong fucker."

"It's what I eat, makes me strong."

They all laughed, and afterward, Nagy hung around Maurice and he seemed pleased when he was called Maurice's dog.

LATE IN THE DAY, almost dark, flecks of snow still in the air, Maurice and Nagy and I left the company area and met a farmer walking down the road. I told him we were looking for food and drink. He said, "Go to Albert, who likes Americans." He pointed up the hill to a farmhouse.

The snow on the road was packed hard by military traffic. In the surrounding hills and fields the snow was deep and smooth. The trees on the hillcrest were heavy with snow. We followed wagon tracks up the hill and saw chimney smoke from the farmhouse, glimmers of light beneath blackout curtains. Monsieur Albert, tall and burly, met us at the door. He wore a dark turtleneck wool sweater and heavy ridged corduroy trousers and wooden clogs. His dense sandy mustache was winged on both ends.

"Nous sommes Américains," I told him.

"Oui," he said, *"C'est évident,"* and welcomed us in to meet his wife and children, two young boys and sixteen-year-old Jeanelle.

We entered the room in which they dined. They had almost finished eating. There was a long plank table with the residue of their meal in the center of the room. We breathed a cozy aroma of garlic and rosemary and apples and mutton.

< 45 >

We'd come from our slit trenches to this real home with a wood-burning oven fed by oak logs. Maurice said, "Tell him that we who come from hell have stumbled into heaven."

I tried to express our pleasure but my French failed me. Jeanelle chimed in with a halting gradeschool English, a shy, child's voice, offering to translate. She was plump and timid, a plain, blue-eyed girl, with tousled dirty-blond hair, dressed in a fisherman's wool sweater and dark wool skirt, and stockings and clogs like her dad's.

I told Jeanelle we had been living in the snow and just being inside was a great pleasure.

She translated for her father, who urged us to warm up on food and drink. He offered a sampling of his apple orchard—hot cider, cider beer, a potent hard cider. His wife brought out sausage and bread.

Maurice groaned with enthusiasm.

"You like?" Jeanelle asked.

Liked? Loved, he said. The bread, the head cheese, the hard salami, the spiced apple cider, the hard cider—it was food for royalty.

Maurice sang for our supper. He accompanied himself on the harmonica. He blew a tune, sang, blew some more. He picked out songs with some foreign vocabulary, silly, innocuous songs that he twisted so they made a different impression than what they were meant to convey. He sang almost mincingly of the different ways Europeans said "yes"—si, si, oui, oui, ja, ja, da, da—when a simple "yes" would do.

< 46 >

He and Nagy drank fast and were quickly high on hard cider. Albert kept pouring.

Maurice sang "Frère Jacques," first in French—the only French he could speak—and then in a raunchy English version, perhaps invented on the spot. I told him it was childish, to cut it out, but that only set him off. One verse went,

> Are you sleeping, are you sleeping,
> Brother John, Brother John?
> Who's in bed with you, sir?
> Our sister? Then let's do her.
> She's family, she's family.

Albert sang along with the French, beamed at the unintelligible English, urged his wife to join in.

She giggled and refused.

Albert held up a slice of strong cheese on a blade for Maurice's inspection. Maurice breathed deeply. "Ahhh!"

"You like?"

Nagy said, "My buddy will eat anything. He'll eat your cheese, your horse, your cow, your sheep, your daughter, anything."

I told Nagy to shut up.

Maurice complimented Jeanelle on her English.

"I learn in school," she said.

"What else they teach you?"

"I no understand."

"They teach you to conjugate love?"

"Pardon?"

< 47 >

"They teach you fucking?"

"He makes jokes," I said to Jeanelle.

She didn't know English well enough to understand his jokes.

Albert invited us to dine with his family as long as we remained stationed near his farm.

On our way back I told Maurice I didn't like his trifling with these generous, simple people.

"No one's simple, Doc."

I refused to go back to Albert's farm with him and Nagy. He said, "Suit yourself." Now that he'd found Jeanelle he didn't need me to interpret.

A few days later he brought Jeanelle to our company area and paraded her before the men so everyone could see what his foraging had turned up in this frozen country-side. He steered her with a hand at the small of her back, pulling her around for introductions. He handled her in a careless way; she was docile and unresisting, a poor trophy, no tasty dish, no fantasy mademoiselle, just a plump country girl, good enough for Maurice who took what he could get.

For him, all Europe was ours for the taking. Before we were done he tried to get it all—the food, the liquor, the money, the Leicas, the Dresden china, the Lugers, the Swiss watches, the ceremonial blades, the family silver, the women. There was no issue as to how the loot was acquired, whether by barter or cash, by seduction or brazen force.

He ate everything.

• • •

< 48 >

Lucca saw me hanging out with Maurice. "What do you see in that jerk?"

I assured him I didn't take Maurice seriously. "He's for laughs."

"Stay away from him, kid. He's nothing but trouble. Hang around him and it'll rub off."

What I couldn't say to Lucca—we had no language for such notions—was that Maurice had something I wanted. I wanted to be carefree and pitiless, able to cross into forbidden territory. It wasn't a trip Lucca would have understood. I was the aid man—technician fifth grade—assigned to the First Platoon, A Company. Those were my boundaries. He expected me to stick to my station and its duties.

"Would you want someone like him around your sister?"

"I don't have a sister."

"Your mother, then?"

It was a laughable idea, my mother and Maurice. Lucca didn't like it that I laughed. There were times when I felt diminished by Lucca. He had a way of reminding me that I was an inexperienced nineteen-year-old kid. What right did anyone have to consider me a kid? I'd treated the wounded, eased the dying, certified the dead. I had the authority to send men back to salvation or to keep them up front in hell.

Only nineteen years old but I was called "Father" by a dying German soldier. We were near the German border, marching through a bleak, snow-drenched forest. We came to a frozen meadow and someone pointed to the far end of

< 49 >

the meadow. Two German soldiers struggled through snow toward the trees, maybe two hundred yards away. The captain told Rebel to see if he could hit them. Rebel knelt, aimed, fired. One went down, the other made it into the woods. The downed man waved at us and the captain told me to go to him, and I asked for a rifleman to accompany me since I wasn't armed.

"What are you afraid of, Corporal? You're a noncombatant. It's a violation of the Geneva convention to shoot you." Sergeant Lucca intervened and told Rebel to go with me.

The wounded German was no one to fear. I could see as we got close that he was an unlikely soldier, old and fragile, among the dregs the Germans were beginning to shove into combat. He must have been trying to surrender when we spotted him. He didn't have a weapon. He lay twisted around his right leg. He wore a gray wool uniform and cap, his eyes huge, his face pinched and unshaven, his mouth stretched as if shrieks were coming out, but it was a smothered sound, *Ohhhhhh. Ohhhhhh.* He saw the red crosses on my arms and helmet and reached for me and cried, *"Vater!"* Father. A spike of femoral bone was sticking through his trousers. I slit his pants, bared the wound at midthigh. He'd shit small, hard, gray turds—what you might see in the spoor of an animal. The shit had worked itself down near the fracture. The stink was pungent and gagging. I put sulfa powder on the exposed bone, covered it with a compress, tied a loose tourniquet above the wound high on the thigh. He was graying fast, going into

< 50 >

shock. He said, *"Vater, ich sterbe."* Father, I'm dying. I stuck morphine into his thigh. He wasn't eased and I gave him another eighth of a grain. I watched him lapse into shock—lips blue, sweat cold, skin gray, pupils distended, pulse weak and fluttery.

I felt as if I, too, had been shot. I yearned for him to be dead so we'd both be released from his pain.

WHEN MAURICE SAID no one was simple he couldn't have meant the dead. The living are complicated but the dead have been stripped of all meaning.

We saw them coifed in crab-shaped helmets, dressed in gray uniforms, mouths agape, gray teeth, gray hands, worn boots, no identities, indistinguishable one from the other, dead meat, nothing to grieve.

There were times when we'd squat near the dead and break open our packages of K rations and eat the processed ham and eggs and the powdered orange juice. We'd light cans of Sterno under canteen cups and heat the bouillon and the sour coffee and afterward lie exhausted among the dead, heads braced on downturned helmets, a cigarette for those who smoked, feeling neither the misery nor pleasure of being alive, snoozing until Sergeant Lucca prodded us. We were stupefied by the death we'd breathed, and stumbled toward combat clutched by the fear that we, too, could be made simple.

We ate among the dead, slept among the dead, tried to rid ourselves of pity for the dead.

Pity hurt. I felt it in my belly and my heart and my tem-

< 51 >

ples. It tightened my throat and lips and made me gassy. It was a hurt that went on and on, and the only cure for it was to become pitiless.

That's what I wanted from Maurice, the power to not give a fuck.

CAPTAIN ROTH ASKED for a patrol to cross the Sauer and bring out casualties from the front, and Sergeant Lucca chose Maurice and Nagy's squad for the mission. Maybe Lucca hoped Maurice would screw up and be sent back to the stockade. Maurice strapped on his gear, and he and Nagy and six others crossed into Germany ahead of us. The squad leader was killed when they entered a booby-trapped pillbox, and Maurice took over. They returned the next day, Maurice leading the squad.

"He showed us the way," Nagy told us. "He took us in and took us out. The man just don't give a fuck." That was how he understood the source of Maurice's courage. "He just don't give a fuck."

Lieutenant Klamm put Maurice in for promotion to assistant platoon sergeant. Lucca didn't want Maurice as a noncom in our platoon. He considered Maurice an unreliable drunk who had already lost his stripes.

The lieutenant said, "I agree with General Patton, who says, 'I don't trust a man who don't drink.'"

Lucca said, "You don't have to trust a man just because he does."

We liked Lieutenant Klamm. He was from Massillon, Ohio, and before the war had been assistant manager of a

< 52 >

Kroger's market. He had found his true path in the army and had no intention of returning to Ohio. We liked and respected him because there was nothing he asked us to do that he wouldn't try himself. He never dithered; he plunged straight ahead.

He was twenty-nine years old, a few years older than most of his troops. He had tamed his appearance with a brush cut and clipped mustache to give an impression of firm maturity, but he could be lured out of character by Maurice, who had the knack of bringing out the locker-room kid in all of us. After a few beers and some raunchy lyrics, the lieutenant, red-faced and roaring, could behave like a kid. Sober again, he stiffened behind the barrier of rank, slightly pompous and formal.

Maurice sometimes sang for us after chow, and the lieutenant requested offbeat songs like "Hold Tight," and Maurice knew how to satisfy GI desires. He sang "Hold Tight" in a way that insinuated his whole repertoire of eating—frogs, mademoiselles, whatever else provoked his appetite. He sang "My Favorite Dish, Fish," with such lewd emphasis that the lieutenant cracked up. Did we understand what Maurice meant by fish? "Fish, fish," the lieutenant said. "Get it?" He didn't spell out the innuendo. He passed on the hint of edible sex with a guffaw and an elbow in the ribs, as though he were passing on a laughable absurdity rather than news of his own unconfessed hunger.

The lieutenant pushed the promotion, and by the time we moved out of reserve and crossed the Sauer, Maurice had recovered three of his lost stripes.

< 53 >

Dear Mom and Dad,

My French is improving. Have contacted the natives and they are friendly. I've eaten the local cuisine, which is a great improvement over our rations. Terribly cold. One of the worst winters on record. My buddy Sergeant Lucca made me a face mask and that helps keep me warm. I'd appreciate more salamis and honey cakes. They make me popular with the boys. Will soon be in Germany to liberate our people.

Love, Leo

By that time I wasn't thinking of a world that extended beyond my platoon. The men of my platoon had become my people. I had lost sight of others.

< 54 >

CHAPTER 4

‹ ACROSS THE RIVER ›

Late one afternoon, the day warming, snow melting, we stripped our packs, dumped surplus gear into jeeps, and moved from reserve.

Trucks brought us to a mushy field outside a river town. The quartermaster handed out supplies to be carried to units up front. There were mortar and bazooka shells, rifle and machine-gun ammo, grenades, medical supplies, rations. Everyone, except officers and noncoms, was loaded down. Billy, who seemed made for bearing, hoisted a case of thirty-caliber ammo. Nagy carried mortar shells. Van Pelt, slight, almost girlish, staggered under a box of C rations. He complained that it was too much, he'd never make it. Lucca said, "You'll make it. Everyone's going to make it. I'll see to it."

We waited till night to enter the ruined town.

Shells whooped in, hot after each other, slamming the stone buildings that lined the river. Traffic massed in the side streets—jeeps, tanks, tank destroyers, weapon carriers, command cars, ambulances, three-quarter-ton trucks, two-and-a-half-ton trucks. MPs crouched in doorways near the intersections, controlling traffic with taped flashlights.

Lieutenant Klamm moved from squad to squad. He told us we were waiting for an artificial moon to rise and light our way across the pontoon bridge and through the minefields on the other side.

Nothing in that sound-blasted night made sense. If they claimed to make moons I wouldn't have been surprised to see a full moon rise at command.

Phosphorous shells lit up the dark hills across the river. The phosphorous blossomed white and intense then slowly faded.

Far to the rear, two searchlights ignited and thrust a giant V against the cloud-choked night sky. The reflected light revealed the path on the other side of the river. That was our moon. MPs waved flashlights like semaphores. "Go! Go! Go!" and the crossing began.

The vehicles went first, followed by artillery. When our turn came we moved onto the bridge with our loads. We jammed up and the lieutenant yelled at us to keep our intervals.

We could hear the river beneath us, pontoons groaning. Shells crossed overhead, ours going out, theirs coming in. We saw the skeleton of the old bridge upstream.

On the other side the vehicles turned onto the river road while we headed straight into the hills. The men struggled with their loads as we started climbing.

Billy climbed in front of me, the case of ammo first on his left shoulder, then his right, then in his arms, his rifle

< 56 >

slung over his shoulder. He wavered from one side of the trail to the other. Lucca told him to keep going. "Show 'em what a rebel's made of."

They wanted us at the top before dawn and we scrambled without stops. Van Pelt, who was struggling, begged for a break. He'd lost the job as messenger when the captain was found going under his covers and had been returned to his role as rifleman. He was frail; the pace was killing him. Lucca told him to shut up and keep moving. Van Pelt fell into step alongside me. He said, "Get me out of this, Leo." I told him I couldn't. He pleaded with me to be sent back. He was never meant to be a foot soldier. He'd had a job in headquarters. He'd offended the captain through no fault of his own and now he was up front. "I can't do this, Leo. You got to get me out."

I stepped up my pace to get away from him.

A quarter mile up the hill, he dropped his load and knelt down. He said, "I can't." Lucca said, "Yes, you can," and started kicking him, sharp jabs to thighs and hips. I bent for Van Pelt's load but Lucca shoved me away.

"You do your job, he'll do his." He told Van Pelt, "I'll kick you to the top if I have to."

Van Pelt, weeping, picked up his load.

"He doesn't belong here," I told Lucca.

"Nothing belongs here. Not you, not me. They use fake moons. Tough shit."

WE REACHED THE summit before dawn, dropped off the supplies, and moved into the forest. B Company had passed through the day before and the ground was littered

< 57 >

with used ammo and abandoned gear and discarded toilet tissue and empty ration cartons. Shells with delicate snouts had exploded in the trees, raining shrapnel straight down. The trees were bared and splintered, tops sheared away. We passed four GIs standing in an uncovered foxhole, braced against the sides of the hole, rifles still aimed toward the front, all dead, one cut off at the forehead, his brain in the bottom shell of his skull.

We moved through the blasted forest into undamaged woods. Here fir and pine and spruce shot straight up, clear of underbrush, the morning sky only visible in broken pieces.

At some point we entered combat. Small-arms fire came from all directions. German machine guns—burp guns, we called them—fired in distinctive quick bursts. M1s and BARs returned fire. We ran doubled up, trying to stay behind trees. We reached an intersection of narrow paved roads where incoming artillery brought us to a halt. We took cover in the woods and lay there while the barrage intensified. Lucca called me up front. There was a casualty on the other side of the road and I was needed. I waited for a pause in the shelling and ran across. Cooper and Grace were already there. The wounded man was Sergeant Schwarzkopf of the Third Platoon. He lay in the snow off the road, an old-cadre noncom, weathered and ruddy, fast losing color, blood welling from a hole in his throat.

Cooper said, "Nothing we can do."

I squeezed between him and Grace, jammed my gloved thumb into the wound. Blood seeped from his mouth. I pulled my thumb away, blood pulsed from his throat

< 58 >

and spread into the snow. My gloves and sleeves were soaked.

A shell hit close. The captain yelled, "Get out of there!" Cooper said, "He's gone, let's go," and we ran for cover. When the shelling was over we found Schwarzkopf in bloody snow, entirely gray, finished bleeding.

WE MOVED IN LINE with the battalion through the forest—light, crusted snow beneath the trees, the snow more dense in clearings. We were on high ground. C Company was below on our left. Someone from C Company spotted my red cross brassards and called out, "Aid man!"

I yelled that I was with A Company.

"Our medic's been hit and we got a man wounded here."

I was at the rear of the platoon and I don't know if anyone heard me yell that I was going down the hill to C Company. I slid down the icy slope. The wounded GI was propped against the hillside, a plump kid, a beard beginning to come through, tended by a buddy. He squealed, "I'm hit," and pointed to his chest. There was a fleck of blood on his jacket, more on his sweater and shirt and long johns. I pulled his clothes aside. His nipple was sheared off. I sprinkled on sulfa powder, taped gauze over the wound. I told him it wasn't bad, to keep going until he had a chance to get to the aid station, no special trip.

I scrambled back up the hill and saw Nagy and Maurice, the last of A Company, vanish into the trees. I started after them but there was another call from C Company and I slid down the hill again. A skinny GI writhed on the ground, held by two of his buddies. He was hit in

< 59 >

the ankle either by a bullet or shrapnel. I gave him morphine, strapped his boot and ankle in a figure eight, told his
buddies that litter bearers would be along and they didn't
have to hang around. I rushed to get back to A Company
but there was no one in sight. I ran toward the sound of
small-arms fire, not sure where our lines were.

Lucca yelled, "Over here!" He'd come looking for me.
"Where you been?"

"I had casualties in C Company."

"You got casualties at home."

"Their aid man is wounded. They needed help."

"The captain's shot."

We found Captain Roth kneeling behind a tree, sighting
a carbine up and down, left and right. "Take cover," he
said. "There's a sniper out there."

I pulled away his jacket and sweater, his scarf and
pleated olive drab shirt while he scanned the trees for the
sniper. I pushed aside a neck chain with a St. Christopher
medal and cut open the upper sleeve of his long johns.
There was a gouged furrow on his right arm at the shoulder. I swabbed the wound with Merthiolate, dusted it with
sulfa, covered it with a gauze patch.

He asked, "Can I go on?"

Lucca told him no problem, he was fine.

He ignored Lucca and spoke to me, "Can I make it?"

"It doesn't look bad. You're okay."

"Then I'll go on." He straightened his clothes and took
off running. We jogged after him.

"He asks if he can go on," I said to Lucca. "I should have
said, no, Captain Sir. If you drop out we'll be better off."

< 60 >

"Lay off. The man's been shot."

"It's a scratch. He's been hurt worse shaving."

"I don't want to hear this," Lucca said, and stepped up the pace to leave me behind.

IN LATE AFTERNOON we emerged from the forest into the sun and had our first clear view of Germany. We stood on the rim of a spectacular valley, the air crisp and clear. This segment of the border was all hills and valleys, meadows dimly greening around patches of snow, no pillboxes or tank barriers visible.

The lieutenant said, "Welcome to beautiful Germany." He told us to start digging and we dug until the captain came by. He said his shoulder was fine. He told the lieutenant, not looking at me, "The medic says it's no problem, I can keep going."

He ordered our platoon out on patrol. We'd come through the Sauer crossing with light casualties and he wanted to keep it that way. "Locate but don't engage," he told the lieutenant.

I asked Lucca why the whole platoon for patrol. Why not a squad?

"Wouldn't you like it to be a squad."

"Why would I like it to be a squad?"

"Medics don't go out with squads. You could stay home while we did the dirty work."

"There's no use for a medic on patrol," I said. "There isn't time for first aid."

"Did I miss something? Did someone make you the CO? They must have promoted you when I wasn't look-

< 61 >

ing. I thought Captain Roth was in command and you were just the medic."

"Maybe we'd be better off if we switched jobs."

Our resentment for each other had been building. He didn't want to hear my complaints about Captain Roth. He didn't want me carrying Van Pelt's load. He wanted me to stick to my job and follow orders. I wanted him to recognize how good a job I was doing and to get off my back. We were tired and hungry and sick of each other.

Lucca moved to the front of the patrol and I stayed at the rear.

THE DAY WARMED. We stripped off gloves and scarves and sweaters and jammed them into our pistol belts. We patrolled along a hillcrest, valley on our left, forest on our right. Lucca told us to stay spread out, no talking, equipment muffled. Krauts were said to be everywhere. After an hour we'd seen no one and the lieutenant finally said, "Okay, let's call it a day."

He reported to the command by walkie-talkie that we'd ranged the company perimeter without sight of the enemy. The captain said, all right, come on home. We dropped our gear and opened our rations and took our first break. Then a scout came running to report a pillbox on the hillside below.

WE LAY IN a platoon front behind two strands of barbed wire at the forest edge. The pillbox was a small concrete bunker fifty yards down the flank of the hill.

< 62 >

There were no apparent defenses, no tank traps or coils of barbed wire, no evidence of mines or guns.

The lieutenant asked Lucca, "Why not take it?"

"The order was to reconnoiter, not engage."

"We don't know what we got here. Could be it's just a storage facility, not occupied."

The lieutenant called the command post to report our find. "Not formidable," we heard him tell the captain, "the size of a large shed, only a couple strands of wire between us and the pillbox, no need for a full-scale assault."

The captain said, "Then take it."

We were armed with rifles, grenades, a BAR, a bazooka, a light machine gun. We lacked the equipment for storming pillboxes—no flamethrowers or explosives or artillery.

Lucca said, "Let's give them a chance to surrender. At least we'll find out if anyone's home."

"Who knows the command for surrender?"

"The medic speaks German."

I had had a year of college German and "surrender" wasn't in my vocabulary. I put together what I thought might serve. I told the lieutenant, *"Geben sie auf."*

"Geben sie auf?"

"It sounds right."

"Let's try it."

The lieutenant stepped over the wire into the open. He funneled his hands around his mouth and shouted, *"Geben sie auf!"* There was no answer and he shouted again, *"Geben sie auf!"* After a couple of minutes he repeated the call. *"Geben sie auf!"*

< 63 >

Finally a small door opened in the side of the pillbox. A tall, paunchy German unfolded through the opening, unarmed and helmetless. He had limp, mousy hair, wore a shoddy gray uniform.

"Geben sie auf!"

He was forty or fifty yards away and must have heard but he paid no attention. He turned to face the pillbox, unbuttoned, pissed, buttoned up, and stooped to reenter. The lieutenant yelled, Son of a bitch! and then something like, Charge! Everyone but me charged over the wire into the field, all weapons firing, rifles, carbines, BAR, light machine gun. I stayed pressed to the ground and didn't budge.

A slide opened in the dome of the pillbox. A stubby gun muzzle emerged. It made a sound like a play gun—*pop, pop, pop.* A line of explosions crossed the platoon front. The countryside ignited. Tracers came at us from surrounding positions. Someone called, "Aid Man!" The men tumbled past me back into the forest. Powell, who carried the BAR, lay on his back, twenty yards from the wire. I ran for him, marked with red crosses on shoulders and helmet to show I was a noncombatant. Long lines of tracers came at me anyway. I dived for Powell. I lay on my belly in slushy snow to check him out. I couldn't feel his pulse or breath. There was no blood. I couldn't find the wound. He was a big man, beefy, with a serene moon face. I tried dragging him but he wasn't easily dragged. Maurice crawled over to help.

"Where's he hit?"

"I don't know. I think he's dead."

< 64 >

We pulled him to the wire. Lucca waved to me from the other flank of the platoon, motioning me to come fast.

"Turner's out there." He pointed toward the right flank.

I spotted Turner, a skinny, gloomy, humorless kid who always feared the worst. He lay at the bottom of a rise off to the right. I ran and hit the ground and crawled to him. There was blood on his chest and I opened his jacket and shirt. His chest was punctured. I crammed gauze into the wound. We carried him into the woods where the platoon had reassembled.

Lucca checked the platoon.

"Where's Billy?"

Maurice pointed toward the pillbox. Billy Baker was still out there, crouched at the base of the pillbox, right where he should have been if he were carrying a butterfly charge, in plain view to us but invisible to the Germans.

Lucca yelled at him not to move but with shells hitting everywhere, who could hear? "That asshole bed wetter! He's done for if he comes into the open. The whole kraut army's zeroed in."

Shells hit every part of the field we'd just abandoned. A few passed overhead and landed in the trees behind us.

The lieutenant called Captain Roth on the walkie-talkie and described our position. "He wants us out. Right now. No more casualties."

"What about Billy?"

"Tell him to stay put. We'll come for him after dark."

Lucca yelled to Billy, "Stay where you are!"

We couldn't tell if he'd heard. Lucca patted the ground to signal him to stay put. "We'll come for you after dark!"

< 65 >

The lieutenant hustled the platoon out of there. Lucca and two others remained to help me with the wounded.

I decided Powell was dead and we left him.

We snapped ponchos over a frame of rifles to serve as a litter for Turner. The brush was thick and there was only room for two of us to carry him and we traded off. We worked around trees and through brush, got stuck, wrestled free. The improvised litter folded and sagged. Turner spasmed, groaned, made no other sound. It was after dark when we reached the company. Litter bearers waited for us.

Lucca wouldn't give us a chance to rest. "Let's go back for Billy."

I said Billy was safe where he was and we'd do better if we waited till daylight.

"I told him we'd come for him. We're going back now."

Six of us went back for Billy.

There was no moon and we could move in the open, but the night terrain was unfamiliar and it took almost two hours to reach the pillbox. On the way we heard traffic in the valley—tank treads grinding, motors of big trucks, the sound of troops on the march.

The pillbox looked bigger at night, a dark hunkered-down space, nothing visible. I couldn't find the spot where I'd left Powell. Lucca called Billy keeping his voice down but there was no answer. He told us to wait while he crawled to the pillbox. He came back alone. "Let's look for him in the woods."

We spread out and thrashed through the woods calling

< 66 >

Billy in tense whispers. It was possible they'd found him and he was in their hands. Or he could have taken off after dark and been settling down for chow while we were still hunting for him. We returned to the company but he wasn't there.

The lieutenant entered him in the morning report as missing in action. He told us the pillbox was our dawn objective. This time the full company would be with us on the assault, our platoon in the lead.

Lucca was bitter that we'd left Billy. He said that we shouldn't have left him. He shouldn't have been with us in the first place. How could anyone have allowed the dimwit up front? The poor jerk should have been reassigned to a rear echelon.

I told Lucca, "I tried. He wouldn't go."

"Why give him a vote when he doesn't operate with a full deck? Just tell him he's going to spend the war in Paris or the States or back on the farm—anywhere but here. You don't give a dummy like that a choice."

Lucca had been riding me all day. I told him if he didn't like the way I did things he could ask battalion aid for a new medic.

Lucca took a deep breath. "For better or worse you're our medic." He grinned when he said it but he wasn't friendly.

"You think maybe it's for worse?"

He paused, then said grudgingly, "If I didn't think you did a good job, you wouldn't be here."

He took off to check on the platoon and get briefed for the morning action and I dug alone, full of resentment. I dug

< 67 >

a few inches, ate K rations, lay down in the shallow trench, but couldn't sleep. I feared what was coming in the morning.

I didn't see Lucca until we assembled before dawn.

WE LEARNED IN the morning that Captain Roth had checked into the battalion aid station to have his wound tended and hadn't returned. He saved his almost unblemished skin and let Captain Dillon from battalion headquarters take over.

Dillon was a taciturn man, in combat since Normandy. He'd been elevated from the ranks through battlefield promotions. He listened to Lieutenant Klamm's account of the valley fortifications and decided the coming action was more than our company could handle without support. He called for artillery and armor.

The shelling started at dawn.

En route to the pillbox we were joined by a tank destroyer, the long barrel of a ninety-millimeter gun jutting from its front.

THIS TIME I found Powell. He was still at the wire, on his back, big and serene, getting the rest we all needed, his wound now clearly visible. A deep depression in his temple had turned purple, evidence I hadn't left him there alive.

LIEUTENANT KLAMM STEPPED across the wire into the field and again called for surrender.

"Geben sie auf!"

His accent was wrong, but this time he was backed by a

< 68 >

big gun. When the pillbox didn't answer he signaled to the tank destroyer and the ninety-millimeter cut loose. We braced against the blast and recoil. Pits of raw concrete opened in the skin of the pillbox. A few rounds were enough. A white cloth flapped from the door. A soldier cautiously emerged, waving the white cloth. We broke into cheers until we saw that it was a GI, not a German, coming out. And not any GI, but our own Billy Baker.

HE'D WATCHED THE Germans leave during the night. They streamed from a railroad tunnel at the base of the hill and he entered after they were gone. The apparently insignificant pillbox was linked to other bunkers and underground barracks and arms depots. We'd been vainly attacking a major fortification of the Siegfried line.

Billy spent the night following tunnels and elevators through the abandoned complex. He returned to the small bunker to sleep and was awakened by the ninety-millimeter rounds hitting the walls.

He had occupied the immense fortress by himself.

The lieutenant put him in for a Silver Star. For all I know it was granted, though he didn't live to get it.

Lucca came up to me afterward and squeezed my arm. "Tough day, kid. We did good." My resentment disappeared in an instant. For his good word I might have considered doing that first day in Germany over again.

I SAW CAPTAIN ROTH weeks later at battalion headquarters, dapper, relaxed, impressively weathered, joking with other brass. I nodded and he nodded back, no need to

< 69 >

salute. He had been reassigned to regimental intelligence and was waiting to receive a major's gold leaf.

Dear Folks,

Have met the Siegfried line. Glad to make its acquaintance but once is enough. Germany is beautiful from a distance. Don't know that I care to see it close-up. You can tell from my jokey tone that I am fine but will be much more improved when that salami arrives. How's Mom's Victory Garden?

Love, Leo

< 70 >

CHAPTER 5

< LUCCA SAID >

Lucca said do your job and don't expect rewards. So what if Billy Baker got a Silver Star for capturing a pillbox? The medal only certified as real an event that never happened. Medals were bullshit. The only thing worth hoping for was to get the job done and go home. Forget the medals. Forget the loot. The rules of war allowed the taking of enemy weapons and gear and battle flags and that sort of thing. Everything else was stealing. If you survived, be grateful. If you came home with eyesight and arms and legs intact that was enough.

Lucca didn't talk much about home. We knew he had a fiancée and that his father was a tailor and the Luccas were a large family but he cut off other discussion of what he was before the war. He kept peacetime apart from wartime. We weren't the people he was going to be with the rest of his life even though we had his full attention right now. Right now he expected everyone to concentrate on finishing the war. He once said to me, bitter over the loot

Maurice Sully was accumulating, "I don't want medals or cameras or knives or guns or someone else's silverware. Let the krauts have it all back once we finish the job."

WE ENTERED GERMANY a village at a time. We assembled before dawn. The assault began when there was enough light. If we were lucky there was no resistance and the villagers lined the cobblestone main street and cheered as if we were their liberators. We shouted, *"Nach Kirche,"* and herded them toward the church, where they waited for a team from Military Government to brief them on occupation behavior. We were free to roam the village and search for weapons, taking whatever we wanted.

Maurice found a complete antique sterling service, hidden under potatoes in the root cellar of a farmhouse. He had an arrangement with the company clerk who had access to our barracks bags, where the loot could be stored.

I heard the clerk complain about the silver Maurice had found. "It's too much," he said. He had to drive the company jeep as far as regimental headquarters to get to our barracks bags. He warned Maurice, "We can get in trouble over this. Enough's enough."

The clerk was a collector of cameras and Maurice offered him a damaged Rolleiflex he'd picked up. The clerk was happy with it. He'd been looking for a Roly. He could get it repaired.

Maurice said, "Enough's never enough," and hunted for loot in every village we entered.

We gave up life in slit trenches when we entered German villages. Two, three, even four of us, in muddy

< 72 >

boots and filthy clothes, shared feather beds in sequestered homes.

THIS IS HOW Maurice acquired his trophy Luger.

A sergeant with Headquarters Company let it be known he would accept a quality Swiss watch in exchange for a mint-condition Luger. Maurice inspected the weapon and craved it. He urged me to heft it and feel its elegance. It wasn't a brutal sidearm like the GI Browning .45, which bore the hand down then hurled it up, the heavy bullet flattening a target even when the hit was far off center. The Luger yearned for the target. It was alive in the hand with a spirit of its own. The grip met the barrel at a rakish tilt with a slight recoil, the thrust straight ahead.

Maurice told the headquarters sergeant, "Hold it for me. I'll get you a watch pronto."

He found the watch in the next Mosel valley town we occupied. A well-dressed elderly citizen with an eighteen-carat Tissot on his wrist was among those being hustled to church. Maurice said, *"Guten Tag."* Good day. The German answered with a relieved smile, *"Guten Tag. Wie gehts, mein Herr?"* How's it going, sir? Maurice had picked up a little German from me. *"Ganz gut, danke."* Very good, thanks, whereupon he stripped the watch and had the wherewithal for the Luger.

I say "found" his Tissot and "found" his Luger and "found" sterling silver and "found" food and drink. It's not as if they were lost or never owned, but to him the wrist that once possessed the watch, the holster that once carried the Luger, were irrelevant in the provenance of these

< 73 >

goods. He saw the watch as though it had never been possessed until revealed to his eyes. It all belonged to him, not only the watch, but the wrist to which it was strapped, and the man whose wrist it was.

In another village, he found a gold Tissot for himself.

Quality weapons and ceremonial blades were at first the collectibles of choice. Later, as Maurice learned value, he looked for jewelry and gems and even art.

THE CAPTAIN TOLD US, "When you hear the order to attack, stand up and start marching and firing and keep marching and firing and don't run, don't hit the ground, don't take cover, don't lose your intervals, always stay in line with the advance. It doesn't matter that you can't see what you're shooting at."

Captain Dillon called this maneuver "marching fire."

When we used marching fire, I had to force myself to rise and start marching. I walked into enemy fire and didn't hit the ground, didn't start digging, didn't wiggle on my belly toward the nearest tree, didn't hug the ground and hide my face. I walked at a steady, modest pace, buddies strung out to the left and right, utterly exposed. It was against all my inclinations. I was as terrified and resentful as if I had been offered as a sacrifice to a god in whom I had no faith.

PFC VAN PELT got out of the war during marching fire.

We lay on our bellies in a field outside the town, spread out in a company front. We waited for the artillery to be-

< 74 >

gin, then rose up at command and began marching behind a billowing wave of smoke. We fired without aim, relying on the intensity of the fire to keep the enemy pinned down.

I followed to the rear and center where I could see both wings of the platoon. The terrain dipped, the squad on the left sank from view, I shifted to keep them in sight. The squad rose up and I moved toward the center. That's when I saw Van Pelt crawling toward me. I yelled, "On your feet! No hitting the ground!" It was none of my business, but his cowardice was tempting and I hated him for showing me how easy it would be to grovel and hide. He crawled to me, rolled over on his back, and said, "Fix me." He'd been hit three times by a burst from a machine gun, in the side below the ribs, then through the fleshy part of the shoulder, then the right cheek, that bullet exiting beneath his left eye, ripping the left cheek. I asked him to move a little to get out of the line of fire. He wiggled over, entirely calm. His eye was closed and I couldn't see how bad the damage was. I gave him morphine, used a triangular bandage to wrap his head and face.

He asked if he was going to die. I said not if he willed to live. He said, "I'm going home then. I will it."

I left him for the litter bearers and ran to catch up with the platoon. We marched and fired all the way to the edge of town. The barrage of smoke lifted and we saw the enemy cowering in trenches below us. They never raised their heads and it was slaughter. Afterward we poured through the town. I found Lucca and Lieutenant Klamm at the town center, waiting for the platoon. The squads arrived garlanded with captured sidearms and gear. Lucca

< 75 >

asked about Van Pelt. I said he'd live, but his Dutch pretty-boy looks were done for.

We heard an explosion from a small bank off the square while waiting for the last of the platoon. It sounded like a grenade.

Maurice and Nagy came from the bank, cramming deutsche marks into a rucksack.

The old deutsche mark was worthless to us. Our exchange currency was the occupation mark.

Lucca wanted to report what he'd seen to the lieutenant.

"It's him or me," Lucca said. "I don't want him in my outfit."

I argued against reporting Maurice. The marks weren't worth the paper they were printed on and with the whole country blowing up who cared if a small-town bank got hit?

In our billet that night I saw Maurice and Nagy sorting the banknotes.

Nagy asked, "What you looking at?"

"Let him look," Maurice said. "He's our buddy. He won't talk." Buried among the worthless German marks I saw gems and gold. I didn't want to see what I felt obliged not to report and turned away.

IT WAS ALMOST SPRING, a breezy, sunny day. We crouched in a pale green meadow, watching chemical mortars set fire to a village. It was still burning when we entered. The only casualties were two elderly farmers, one gored by a bull he was trying to lead from fire, his right buttock ripped open. I pulled the flesh together with over-

< 76 >

lapping strips of butterflied adhesive but couldn't close the gap and covered it with large gauze compresses. The other farmer was almost entirely burned, clothes seared to his skin, a burly old man, hair crisped, skin hanging from his jowls, hands and arms blistered and blackened. He suffered in a language I didn't understand while three of us worked on him—me, and Cooper, and Grace. We cut away as much of his clothing as we could, put him on a clean sheet on a kitchen table, slathered him with burn ointment. I worked on his legs, Grace on his torso, Cooper on his head and face. Litter bearers hauled him away in a jeep.

Maurice made up a song in waltz time about the burned farmer. One verse went,

> We took this town to gather loot
> and smoked a Kraut like a cheroot.
> His farmyard smelled of spring and hell,
> Manure, new grass, and burning gel.

On the way to our billet we passed a tankman, stained with grime, goggles raised over his helmet, standing at the open door of a burning house, rolling drunk, a bottle of wine in one hand, guiding his piss with the other. A GI, foraging for dinner, chased a squawking hen in front of our billet.

That evening Cooper, the Second Platoon medic, negotiated with a compliant fräulein. He offered cigarettes and D-ration chocolate for what she had to trade. He would have added soap and toilet paper, but cigarettes and chocolate were enough. Cooper, a handsome, easy-talking

< 77 >

Southerner, didn't speak German and his English was sometimes so drawled I had to concentrate to unravel its sense. Yet in the brief hour after we entered the village he located the woman, jollied her into accepting his terms, set her up in a barn loft to wait on him and his buddies. He rattled on with "y'alls" and "honeys" as though he were speaking to an Alabama woman. He laughed constantly while he chatted her up. He invited me to join him and Grace and I met her lying in fragrant hay, her skirt hiked, a sturdy farm girl in heavy dark dress and a man's boxer shorts and grass-encrusted boots.

Cooper saw my reluctance and said, "You go first." He and Grace withdrew down the ladder to await their turn.

I lay beside her without desire and didn't touch her. I wanted the respect of my buddies, relief from dread, not much else.

"You'll like her," I told Cooper when he asked how she was.

The fräuleins lacked cigarettes, soap, sweets. There was little fresh meat. Everything was in short supply. *Alles kaput.* They were ready to trade sex for cigarettes or D-ration chocolate bars or sticks of *Kaue Gummie* or K rations or bar soap or combinations of these commodities, depending on the strength of GI desire and fräulein resistance. It was convenient to believe that these were farm girls, familiar with animal nature, and that their own animal nature was no problem to them. The truth is few of us examined our beliefs. We took what war offered us.

Lucca said to me glumly, "Just make sure you're not trading for clap."

< 78 >

CAPTAIN DILLON HAD announced a theaterwide nonfraternization policy, regulating all dealings between German civilians and GIs. Minimum contact. *Guten tag, danke, bitte, nach Kirche,* etcetera, no hanky-panky with fräuleins.

VD was epidemic among the troops. Whole companies were decimated by clap. A fifty-dollar fine for anyone caught fraternizing. Captain Dillon told the men he was talking about serious business—sterility, blindness, madness. If we were willing to do business with the fräuleins and risk the fine then we'd better take precautions.

Maurice said sex was less risky than war. He'd rather be crazy than dead.

We approached a village on the way to the Rhine. The battle ahead was stalled and we crouched on both sides of a gully that led into town, waiting for the action up ahead to be finished. We heard small-arms and mortar fire. The word came back that the village had been decked out in white flags, apparently surrendered, when a German sniper killed a popular Second Platoon noncom.

That was the excuse for what followed.

A private from the Second Platoon, a skinny Louisiana kid with a freckled, burned face named Roy Jones, brought back two German prisoners who may have been snipers. He marched them down the gully, between our columns. The prisoners were about thirty or forty feet from me, arms stretched overhead. One was very tall, the other very short. The tall one was bareheaded, with grayish-blond hair. The short one wore an overseas cap. They both wore gray uniforms, trouser legs tucked into boots. Jones took aim. I

< 79 >

said, "Oh, no," not loud enough. The first shot somehow missed and the Germans continued marching, arms raised. The next shot bowled over the short one. The tall soldier took three more steps before he, too, was shot down.

I put myself in the shoes of the tall German soldier, marching down the gully, his hands in the air, a few steps in advance of Jones. I couldn't forget how he kept marching after Roy Jones killed the little man alongside him. He took three steps at the same pace as when two of them had marched in front of Jones, no wavering—one, two, three, then *crack*. When he collapsed, his head fell a little faster than the rest of him, his arms—still elevated—floated down. He hit the ground like a carcass dropped to a block for butchering.

Maybe he had continued marching because spirit or consciousness no longer guided him. Or maybe up till the last second he hoped Jones would relent.

I came to know Roy Jones when he later joined our platoon. What he'd done made him more than he otherwise seemed: a mere country boy with parochial judgments, a fool, no one you'd listen to but for his terrible possibilities.

I told Lucca I didn't want to be part of what Roy Jones had done and considered asking for a transfer from the company.

Lucca said death was everywhere. Where would I go to avoid it?

I asked if we were no better than the Germans.

Lucca was tired of his obligations, tired of the war, tired of his men, tired of me. "Let's just get it over with," he said.

< 80 >

SOMETIMES OUR OBJECTIVE was the high ground. The German village was picture-postcard lovely from the vista of the high ground. You could see it in its entirety, centered around a church, homes tightly gathered about a town square, plowed fields spreading from the edges, the whole ringed with forest, tidy and compact. Before battle you might hear the distant medley of cattle lowing, dogs barking, church bells chiming. Later, in the spring, you smelled the newly turned soil and manured fields. It was the sound and smell of a world you might find in your best dreams.

Despite the great view, the high ground was not a place to be. Enemy artillery concentrated on the high ground.

At first I tried being casual about artillery fire. Shells would hit in the distance then move in, and it seemed humiliating to rush for cover, so I took my time getting out of the way, waiting almost for the warmth of the blast before jumping into my slit trench. It didn't take long to find out what shrapnel could do and then I hit the ground sooner rather than later, not worried about looking foolish.

A shell fragment could act as bullet, knife, cleaver, bludgeon. It could punch, shear, slice, crush. It could be surgical in its precision or make sadistic excess seem unimaginative.

The more experienced I was, the edgier I became. By the time the war ended, any loud noise could bring me down.

IT WAS ON HIGH ground that the war reached its climax for me.

< 81 >

We dug in above a Mosel valley village. Billy and I did most of the digging. Lucca was busy checking positions. We dug fast and, once safe underground, ignored the occasional shell. We dozed till late afternoon when the sound of battle stopped. We watched B Company enter the village without resistance. It was a lovely sight from the high ground, the tidy village in the late afternoon of a crisp, sunny day, the troops of B Company sauntering down both sides of a country lane into town. Lucca told us to buckle up, we were joining B Company. "Hot chow tonight. Let's go," almost the last words he spoke. We left our trenches, strapped on our gear. Maurice pointed into the distance. He shouted, "Rockets!" I don't know what he saw, perhaps rockets coming off the launcher a mile away. We called the rockets "screaming meemies," didn't take them as seriously as cannon fire. They hadn't proved as accurate. Instead of the whistling sound of artillery shells passing overhead, the rockets shrieked by in bundles. Once you learned the sound there wasn't much to fear. The rockets had never come close and it was only because I was spooked by shell fire that I dived for the slit trench as soon as Maurice called out, "Rockets!" I was still in the air when the rocket hit and the shock turned me in midair and I landed on my back inside the trench. Lucca flopped on top of me. I started laughing at the close call. Lucca cried, "Help me, Leo." Billy lay at the edge of the trench. He cried, "Morphine." I wiggled out from under Lucca. He said, "My stomach." I opened his jacket. His belly was slit open, rolls of intestine exposed. Billy's leg was gone at the upper calf, the stump bleeding. I yelled for help, grabbed a

< 82 >

belly compress from my kit and pressed Lucca's gut back in. A lieutenant from the Second Platoon came over, looked at Billy, said, "I can't." I jumped out, tied a tourniquet above the knee, stuck Billy with morphine, climbed back into the trench. The rockets screamed in, salvo after salvo. They kept coming. The company got out of there fast. Lieutenant Klamm yelled at me to stay until they could send help. A second platoon rifleman jumped in with us. He squeezed himself into a ball to take up as little room as possible in the crammed trench. I suppose he was there to protect us. Lucca whispered, "My leg." His ankle was loose. The foot wobbled when I touched it. I used his bayonet and scabbard to splint the foot and ankle. I covered Billy with a raincoat, loosened the tourniquet. He said nothing more after he called for morphine. The night sky was lit by rockets. The Germans seemed to be coughing up everything they had left. The rockets screamed in for hours. Lucca moaned once, "Mama, Mama," but didn't answer when I asked how he was doing. The rifleman never said a word.

It was deep night before the barrage ended. A jeep came up the hill with Lieutenant Klamm and two litter bearers. I told Lucca he was going to the hospital but he didn't respond. I thought I felt Billy's breath but couldn't catch his pulse. We placed them on litters across the cab of the jeep and it took off.

Lieutenant Klamm led us to the village. Our platoon was in the kitchen of the company billet. There were men under the table, on top of the table, on the sink, under the sink, crouched against the tile oven, on top of the oven. I

< 83 >

told them about Billy and Lucca. Lucca was still alive. I wasn't sure about Billy.

The next day we learned that the ambulance carrying them to the division hospital was caught in a jam of military traffic and that they died en route.

Maurice gave me brandy in a canteen cup. I told him exactly what I saw, the neat coils of intestine bulging from Lucca's slit belly, his ankle so loose it must only have been attached by skin and ligaments. Lucca's last word was "Mama." Billy's last word was "morphine." I drank the brandy and lay down but didn't sleep.

I felt no fatigue or grief. I was intensely awake. I felt I understood the last moment of the tall German whom Roy Jones killed. I could be in the shoes of the man about to die and march ahead and feel death coming and be calm and resigned.

In the morning Lieutenant Klamm told me I was wanted at company headquarters and to bring my gear.

"What for?"

"Can't say."

Captain Dillon met me at the company jeep. He said, "Congratulations," and shook my hand. I was among a handful selected from the regiment to inaugurate a new program of battlefield leaves to begin immediately. The jeep would take me to regiment and I'd be on my way to Paris.

Sergeant Lucca was mistaken when he said there were no rewards. He just didn't know how to go about getting them.

< 84 >

CHAPTER 6

‹ PARIS LEAVE, 1945 ›

Blustery weather, rain flung in my face, the sky moving fast, brief moments of clearing, then black clouds again and rain.

The muddy jeep took me to regimental headquarters. I joined eleven others in the carriage of a three-quarter-ton truck and we were driven to division headquarters. There we transferred to a two-and-a-half-ton uncovered truck, and thirty more GIs climbed aboard. It started raining again; we broke out ponchos and huddled together for the two-hour drive to a supply depot, a vast tent city outside Esch in Luxembourg. We were led to a storeroom where we received new outfits, everything from long johns to boots and hip-length field jackets. I surrendered my own bloody jacket with the last traces of Lucca and Billy Baker on the sleeves.

We carried our new clothes and filed naked down a maze of canvas corridors that ended in overhead showers. We left clothes and boots in an adjoining dressing tent, stood on duckboards over mud, and showered amid squalls of rain. We dried, shaved, dressed, were shepherded to a great tent set up with plank tables and benches. Hundreds of us moved down a chow line, mess kits extended for turkey and stuffing, cornmeal biscuits, apple pie. Afterward we marched to paymasters who doled out three months' back pay in francs and dollars. At midnight we climbed aboard a hissing train and entered dimly lit compartments, blackout shades covering the windows. We sat four to a bench, facing each other. The train, steaming and ready to go when we climbed aboard, didn't budge for two hours. Then it lurched, picked up pace, and began to travel at a good clip only to grind to a halt just beyond Esch. We were dragged backward and shunted to a siding. We waited another hour while priority traffic passed.

From the beginning I had an acute sense of time slipping away. I wanted to get far enough from the front to be beyond recall by some clerk who might discover that the leave was a mistake. The redheaded corporal seated next to me said, "Fuck this waiting. The leave begins as of now." He pulled out an unlabeled pint bottle, drank, and passed it to me. "So long, Sobriety. Drink and pass it on." He introduced himself. "For some goddamn reason they call me Red."

Red was short and solid with a sharp face and receding chin. He spoke with a rural twang spiked with inappropriate giggles. "I promised my buddies, no sleep and no waking minute sober." He was here, he said, because his outfit was caught by artillery in the forest outside of Metz. Tree bursts sprayed shrapnel straight down. They tried digging in but the ground was dense with roots so they axed trees

< 86 >

and laid down two courses of midsized logs under a log roof. His entire squad crawled under the shelter, the roof so low they couldn't rise to their knees. They lay inside on their bellies, coming out only to piss and shit and get rations and serve guard duty. They were blasted continuously for a week. "Loudest show on earth," he said, and giggled. Most of the casualties happened during the brief periods they were outside their log pens.

He showed me his net-covered steel helmet, one side gashed open. He intended to keep the helmet as a memento of the forest. Eight dead, twelve wounded in his platoon. He was one of three survivors in his squad. Surviving was his ticket to this special train. He shouted, "I earned this fucking leave," as if someone had challenged his being here, then giggled. He considered himself a representative of everyone in his platoon and meant to use his leave for their pleasure as well as his. He repeated his vow against sleep and sobriety. His destination was Pig Alley and around-the-clock whoring.

We all told stories to justify being on leave from the front. When my turn came I told how Lucca dived for the trench a fraction of a second behind me, his belly slit open. I told how Billy Baker hung over the edge of the trench, his leg blown off at midcalf. I embellished what happened and made it false, Lucca larger than life, Billy distorted by maudlin sympathy. An invisible, alien country passed on the other side of opaque train windows, and yearning to be located, I betrayed an as yet unfathomed experience to win the sympathy of strangers.

We reached the Gare St. Lazare in early morning and

< 87 >

descended into a huge shed, a skeleton of iron beams and struts supporting an acre of glass roof. Trucks carried us through a gray drizzle to the Grand Hotel, its grandness reduced to barracks, the lobby transformed into a mess hall. The rooms were all doubles, and Red and I teamed up. We entered an almost bare room furnished with cots. I flopped onto my bed and Red said, "Uh, uh. No lying down. Keep moving, Buddy. We sleep on the way back."

I told him to go ahead. I'd use the john and meet him in the mess. He left and I lay down and tried to go under but after a few minutes forced myself to join the others for breakfast.

They had decided Pig Alley was our destination. It was still early but the plan was to stop at bars en route.

Paris was the first undamaged city I'd seen in months. It was cold and gray and beautiful, ancient stone façades intact. It was the first week of March and the grand boulevards were lined with leafless trees. Though military traffic owned the avenues, and uniforms were everywhere, you could already see the shape of a world at peace.

The city had been liberated for a few months but we were still welcomed at the bars—*Bravo, les Américains*—and the good feeling earned us some free drinks.

Red took it on himself to be our spokesman. I translated but couldn't do justice to his lingo.

"We come from war and we seen everything—'toot' like you say—and you got a beautiful city and there is no woman as beautiful as the mademoiselle. If she was mine I'd keep her under lock and key and I'm grateful to you

< 88 >

garçons for turning the ladies out in the streets where they can be had for a couple bucks."

I didn't try to translate the last.

Red had his eye on the clock, and about noon, he said, "Time for Pig Alley."

I said, "I'll take a raincheck. See you for dinner."

"You're pooping out on us, Buddy."

I told him I'd rather sleep than get laid.

"Your funeral. Fifty-four hours from now you won't have that choice."

I took off for the hotel, entered our room, hoped to sleep as long as it took to stop feeling stunned, but woke up two hours later, still numb and displaced. The day had cleared. It was sunny and warm. I walked on the Champs-Elysées behind elegant women, in arm's reach but as distant as stars. I stopped at a barber shop, couldn't think of the vocabulary for haircuts and let the barber do what he wanted. I found a photographer near the hotel and had my photo taken.

I walked past the Arc de Triomphe and the Opéra, stopped at Napoléon's Tomb, which was closed, took the metro to the Ile St. Louis, went to Notre Dame, vaguely noted the massive buttresses and arches, the stained glass, the statues, the gargoyles, too dazed to focus on anything.

In late afternoon I returned to pick up my photo, a glum, unsmiling twenty-year-old with a fresh haircut, sideburns almost erased, new olive drab wool shirt open at the throat. It was a disappointment. I had hoped to find a face transformed by war. I wrote on the back, "March 3, taken

< 89 >

on leave, two days after the death of Sgt. Edward Lucca, Your son, Leo," and mailed it from the hotel. I walked to the Musée de l'Homme, stood on the balcony, looked down the concourse to the Eiffel Tower, and watched the day darken.

I returned to the hotel with forty-eight hours left.

Back for dinner, Red told me to forget the Eiffel Tower and all the tourist crap. The best sight in town was Pig Alley. He and the other six emerged from the Pigalle metro stop and it was zigzag all the way to the Moulin Rouge. Their goal was the Moulin Rouge but it wasn't yet open. Anyway they didn't make it past the gauntlet of whores. They were taken to hotels, then released to walk the gauntlet again.

Their destination after dinner was again the Moulin Rouge and I joined them. We came out of the metro, passed the long line of women calling their offers, entered the darkened vestibule of the Moulin Rouge. Red pulled aside the blackout curtain and exposed a vast, turbulent room. There were Russians, French, British, Norwegians, Poles, Moroccans, turbaned Indians. Officers sat at tables next to enlisted men. Waiters squeezed between jammed tables carrying trays of drinks overhead. A band played at the front of the room. The singer, a bare-shouldered, middle-aged blond woman, stood at the mike on the lip of the bandstand singing a throaty, all-out rendering of "J'attendrai."

"J'attendrai. . . ." I shall wait, day and night I shall wait for your return. . . .

A girl, perhaps sixteen or seventeen years old, sat in a straight-backed chair, just inside the entrance, apparently

< 90 >

waiting for someone. She wore a wide-brimmed hat and a suede jacket and a short flowered dress, legs clamped together, stiffly smiling, eyes distant. I said, *"Bonjour."* She smiled but didn't answer. I asked if she spoke English. She said, *non.* I said she was *très belle* and invited her to join us. She smiled and shrugged, *peut-être,* maybe, and remained where she was

We wiggled through a crowd, found a table, ordered champagne. Women came flocking, wearing short dresses, bare-shouldered, black-stockinged, heavily made up, sharply scented. They sat on our laps, hoisted their dresses, showed us garters and bare thighs and florid panties. It wasn't elaborate dealing. *Combien?* Francs, dollars, cigarettes, quicky rates, the cost for the full night. A woman my mother's age sat on my lap and exposed her legs and thighs. She asked my name. I told her and she said, "Zig zig, Léo?" I said, no thank you. She was replaced by another. "Zig zig? Suck suck?" I said, "No, thank you," got up and went back to the girl at the door.

"Je m'appelle Léo," I said, *"un soldat Américain."* She smiled. Her name was Marishka.

"C'est un nom Russe?"

"Oui."

I said it would please me if she would come to our table and sit with me.

Again, she said maybe.

I said I'd wait for her at our table.

We ordered more champagne, the men trying to get even higher before leaving with the women they'd chosen. Red summoned passing women to solicit me.

< 91 >

"Take care of my Buddy, he's shy, *compris?*"

I said, *"Non, merci."*

Red asked, "What's the problem, Buddy? We got three days, not three years."

Marishka came to our table and I grabbed a chair from another table and squeezed her in alongside me.

Red said, "Now this one is worth holding out for."

She was still wearing her hat and jacket. She didn't want a drink. I asked if she would like to show me the city.

"Perhaps," she said.

She seemed too young to be in this place. She claimed she was eighteen, a student at the Sorbonne.

"The Sorbonne? Really?"

"You don't believe me?"

"Of course I believe you. What is it you study?"

"Political science," she said.

I told her I had been a student but my university wasn't so grand as the Sorbonne. It was a university near Detroit. Did she know Detroit?

She shrugged, then abruptly changed the subject. "You would like me to be with you?"

Yes, I would like that.

"Est ce que tu veux zig zig?"

She pulled up her dress, miming her elders. She was beautiful there, too, smooth thighs, a wisp of light pubic hair curling from black panties.

"Combien?"

"Vingt dollars pour la nuit."

"Fine," I said.

< 92 >

She was in a hurry, perhaps forbidden to be in the room, perhaps under age, not licensed.

Red slapped my back as we got up to go. He congratulated me for snatching this beauty from all the competition. The officers would have eaten her up. She could have chosen some flashy Brit or a red-hatted Zouave. But this trophy mademoiselle, a credit to our division, to our squad of eight, chose a T-5 from the Third Army. Red gloated in my triumph as if it were his.

Marishka took me a couple of blocks to the Hotel de l'Avenir, a drab building with a faded gilt sign. A portly woman dozed on a chair in the tiny lobby near the stairs. Marishka paid her and we climbed two flights to a dingy studio with a closet-sized recess containing a bidet and washstand.

"Would you like me to pay you now?"

"Yes, please."

"In francs or dollars?"

"I prefer dollars."

She didn't ask me to wash or put on a rubber. She pulled off her dress, unhooked her brassiere, stepped out of her panties, and offered with full confidence a view she knew would please.

"Tu es très belle."

"Merci."

She climbed under the covers and waited for me to undress.

She was what I'd dreamed of; no, more than I expected. I barely entered her. I came without release. She beamed a child's smile and I didn't know how I could remain the night.

< 93 >

"Listen," I said, "let's try again after I've rested. I'm very tired."

She asked if I wanted to sleep.

"No, just rest."

"Okay," she said. "I'll wash."

There was no washroom door and I could see her sitting on the bidet. She smiled at me, unembarrassed, then standing naked, her back to me, she washed her hands. She bent to wash her face. I could also see her in the mirror. She used a cloth for her underarms. She toweled herself, dabbed on scent, brushed her long brown hair. She burped, said, "Ooh la la!" and smiled.

She was fresh and vibrant, there was nothing her body did that was less than beautiful. But when she was in my arms I lost heart again and was drained by my coming. It wasn't what I'd hoped for or what her beauty deserved. She was receptive, not transported. There was the rest of the night still waiting, my leave diminishing in her bed.

I used what French I had easily, without self-consciousness, able to say what I wanted to say. I said it was difficult to believe she was a student at the Sorbonne. Perhaps she had attended a lecture.

Why was it hard to believe she was a student?

I couldn't understand why a student at the Sorbonne would earn a living off soldiers at the Moulin Rouge.

She asked if I had any idea how hard life was in wartime.

I said, "You're right, I have no idea; I believe you. You are a student at the Sorbonne."

"Yes," she said, "it's true."

< 94 >

I said in English, "Who gives a fuck?"

She asked what I'd said.

"Nothing important."

Her parents were Russian, had left after the revolution, had come to France in 1925. She was born in Paris. She had an older brother who was a prisoner of war in Germany.

I asked if she'd had many men and she said, not many.

She asked if I'd had many women and I said, a few.

She said, "You are also young."

I told her I was here—in Paris—because of what happened to me on the battlefield. Again I told the story I should never have used, how my closest friend, Lucca, fell on me, his belly torn open, and another friend lost his leg, and I stayed with these dying men all night in a hole in the ground. I told her that the night was on fire all around us and I lay as close to Lucca in that hole as she was to me in this bed.

I wanted Marishka to experience the slit trench and the night on fire and Lucca and Billy dying, hoping, I suppose, that if her feeling deepened it would nourish mine, and in fact, there was tenderness in her kisses. I had the illusion my response was heartfelt but the satisfaction didn't last long. I lay beside her uncomforted and ashamed. I had again used Lucca's death to win sympathy.

I asked if we were obliged to lie here all night.

"I don't understand."

"Did I pay to be in bed all night?"

She laughed. Would I like to go out to eat? It would be difficult to find a restaurant so late. There was little to eat

< 95 >

in the restaurants—almost everything was rationed—but she had an idea. The bakers would soon begin baking for the morning and she knew a baker who would let us have fresh bread and coffee. Would I like that?

The *boulangerie* was down the block. Lights were out and she rapped on the window and the baker came to the door, a fat man with heavy jowls and a thick black mustache dusted with flour; he was dressed in white, his hair covered in white. He embraced Marishka, clearly pleased to see her. His French was too fast and I only got the drift of what he said. He loved Americans. The war would soon be over, Paris returned to itself. After this past hard winter, there would be a marvelous spring, and what did I think of Marishka?

"She's beautiful," I said. He led us through the dark shop to the ovens in back, sat us at a small wooden table with spindle legs, and brought out plates. He had a treat for us. He had difficulty getting enough butter so he didn't make croissants every night, but a supply had arrived and we were in luck—hot croissants, fresh sweet butter, marmelade, coffee. He refused to let me pay.

His name was Victor. Like Marishka he had a Russian mother. His father was French, also a baker.

He asked what was my nation.

Les États Unis. Couldn't he tell by my uniform?

Yes, but all Americans came from elsewhere. Where did my parents come from?

"The Ukraine, Zhitomir, near Kiev."

"Marvelous! Congratulations!" We were countrymen.

He brought out a bottle of wine, poured glasses for us.

< 96 >

"Look at the beautiful child," he said, nodding at Marishka who licked a fleck of wine from her lips. "She drinks with her tongue like a cat."

He had to get back to work and gave us a baguette to take with us.

I asked Marishka how much of the night I had purchased. Did I have time left?

She said she was very tired now.

"Let's go back to your hotel."

She would have to pay the concierge again.

"I will pay the concierge. And I will pay for your time tomorrow. I paid twenty dollars for the night? I will pay twenty dollars for the day. Okay?"

"Okay."

"And if I want you for tomorrow night you will accept another twenty dollars?"

"You want me for tomorrow night?"

"Perhaps."

"Then perhaps yes."

"Is it yes to any man with twenty dollars?"

"I choose who I go with."

I gave her another twenty dollars. "Tomorrow is mine. I buy your day. And maybe I will buy tomorrow night also. Agreed?"

She took my arm. "You like me, then?"

"To like you is simple."

We returned to her hotel, undressed, lay in bed. She let me fumble around and held me affectionately. She said she needed to sleep.

Before leaving I asked if she would remember me.

< 97 >

She said, "I see you tomorrow, no?"

"After tomorrow night, when I have gone back to the war, will you remember me?"

"Oh, yes."

"How can you remember me when there are so many others?"

"I will remember you."

"Why?"

"Because you are intelligent, you are young, you are clean. You speak French. You are special. Yes, I will remember you. Why do you want that I remember you?"

I told her everything that happened in these hours had to be important. There was no time to waste on what had no importance. Money, for instance, was not important. Twenty dollars for you is important, I said. Twenty dollars for me is not important.

"Perhaps I should ask for more," she said smiling.

"Listen. I'm going back to my hotel. But tomorrow is mine, no one else can have it. Agreed?"

"Okay."

"So if another American soldier offers you twenty-five or thirty dollars you will say, 'No, I am taken, I belong to another'?"

"You are crazy," she said, "that is why I will remember you."

I told her to meet me outside my hotel at noon. She wouldn't be allowed into the hotel. She should be there exactly at twelve o'clock.

When I was dressed and ready to take off, she asked, "And you will remember me?"

< 98 >

"You took all my dollars. Of course I will remember you."

"Good."

RED WAS SPREAD OUT on his belly, arm dangling from the cot, stripped to his GI underpants, moaning with his mouth open. I went to the bath down the hall and took a bath and when I returned Red was sitting on the edge of the cot, his head in his hands.

He asked what time it was. I said four in the morning.

He told me our schedule. "We leave from the hotel twelve noon, day after tomorrow. That's thirty-two hours. We're due back at our outfits by midnight, another twelve hours." He had the latest battle reports from the army newspaper, *Stars and Stripes.* "A big push to the Rhine, tank battles, lots of action. Just forty-eight hours from now we'll be assembled for a morning assault. So what the hell am I doing in bed?"

He got up, pulled on his clothes, combed his hair, straightened his cap.

He asked, "You coming?"

"I got to sleep. I'll be crazy if I don't sleep."

He implored me to come party with him. He wanted to find *his* Marishka. My French would help. There were beautiful mademoiselles everywhere and somewhere one for him. "Don't let me down, Buddy. We're running out of time. Let's party."

"Not a chance."

He said once more, "Come on, Buddy," and I wanted him out of the room and blew up and told him to quit call-

< 99 >

ing me buddy, my buddies were dead, he was no buddy of mine, to hell with the buddy bullshit anyway.

He held up his hands as if warding off blows. "Okay, okay, okay."

I immediately apologized. "Give me a couple hours and I'll go with you."

He giggled. "Sleep, Buddy. You earned it. Now I got to go out and earn mine."

I READ *STARS AND STRIPES* over a breakfast of coffee and powdered eggs and Spam. There was a battle along the whole of Germany west of the Rhine. Something enormous was happening. My platoon was dying while I dallied in Paris.

I had the same need as Red to make these hours extraordinary. I didn't look forward to Marishka. That was killing time. I wouldn't have been unhappy if she hadn't been waiting for me at noon, but there she was beneath the naked chestnut tree, across from the hotel entrance. She waved, *"Bonjour, Léo."*

It was chilly and overcast and she wore a head scarf and a GI raincoat and carried a folded umbrella.

I asked where she'd found the raincoat. She said a friend had given it to her.

"An American friend?"

"Yes."

"People give you things because they are friendly?"

"Yes, that is true."

"I'm friendly but I have no more to give. You have it all."

< 100 >

She ignored the belligerence and asked if I'd slept well.

"Comme ci, comme ça."

Did I want to rest?

There would be time to rest. I wasn't looking for rest.

Did I still want to see Paris?

I didn't know what I wanted.

If I would like to walk we could go down to the river or take the metro to the Bois de Boulogne or go to the Luxembourg Gardens.

Walking didn't interest me. I had done too much walking.

Would I care to visit the Sorbonne?

Again my French failed me and I couldn't describe my mood. The word *"désespoir"* seemed fancy. *"Chagrin"*— grief—would have led me back to Lucca and another betrayal. Maybe sleeplessness would explain enough. She seemed even more like a kid, her hair pulled in tight by the scarf, her nose made prominent, her smile shy and anxious. She looked dumpy in the raincoat.

"We can go to a café and talk," she said.

Speaking French had become an effort. I wasn't doing as well as the night before. I told her I wasn't good company.

"You don't want to be with me?"

I said, "I paid, didn't I?" then apologized. I told her I was tired and annoyed at having to explain myself.

She said she understood.

We kept walking and passed a movie theater showing Charlie Chaplin's *City Lights.*

I asked if she knew the film.

< 101 >

She had seen *Modern Times* but not this one.

"Do you want to see it?"

She was agreable, and why shouldn't she be? I'd bought her time and it was a way of being with each other without obligation.

The dark, familiar place was the same in Paris as in Detroit. I could detach from her, take a recess, consider what I could do in these next few hours to make my return to combat bearable. My platoon was dying while I killed time in Paris, and that was unbearable.

Marishka was thrilled by the movie. She laughed like a child. At the end, when the once blind girl extends a flower to the tramp and the theme plays—"Won't you buy my pretty violets?"—I, too, was sucked into it. I felt the pressure of tears and was dismayed and held back. She sobbed out loud.

I said, "Shut up," and got up, and she followed me out.

"What is wrong?"

"You cry for that?"

She felt sad for the little tramp who at the end was so alone.

"It's a lie," I said. "The little tramp is a rich man. He has everything. The beautiful ladies adore him. He is never alone. The world explodes"—detonates, I said—"and you don't cry for that but you cry for a character in a film."

"You are right. I will cry no more. You didn't pay to see me cry."

I told her again I didn't care about the money, the money had no importance. Only time had weight for me. I'd pay a fortune to have more time. Twenty-four hours

< 102 >

left. Time was the only thing I truly wanted to own. My time was vanishing.

She got the gist of what I meant despite my messed-up French. "You don't want to go back to the war."

"What good is wanting?"

It started to rain and she opened her umbrella, a uselessly elegant flower of impermeable cloth. She held it over me. I was barely covered and her head was getting soaked. I told her to take the umbrella for herself; I didn't need it.

She said, "Come to my place, where I live. You didn't pay to see me cry. We'll have something to eat."

IT WASN'T A hotel in Pigalle, but an old building near the Seine in the seventh *arrondissement,* and we walked a narrow stairway to the fourth floor and down a bleak corridor into a cramped three-room apartment she shared with a couple she identified as fellow students at the Sorbonne. There was a minuscule kitchen. The fairly large, bright living room belonged to her roommates, Annie and Bernard. There was a bed heaped with pillows and an Oriental rug. The walls were decorated with movie posters— one with Jimmy Cagney and the Dead End Kids, *Les Anges Aux Figures Sales,* Angels with Dirty Faces. There was a battle scene with a bandaged, bloody sansculotte hoisting a red flag. The poster said, "Come, Communards, Meet the Red Sun of May; Come, Communards, Meet the Red Day." The toilet and bath were down the corridor, shared with other tenants.

Her room was tiny and dark, a mattress on the floor, old

< 103 >

photos and etchings on the walls, a beaded lamp on a wood mosaic end table, a cane chair, an ornate gold-framed mirror above the bed. There was no door to her room. Strings of beads separated her from her roommates. She said we didn't have to worry about being interrupted. They were at work and wouldn't return till morning. I sat at a small table in the kitchen while she heated a large iron pot on a gas burner. She brought out bread from a window box. Rid of scarf and raincoat, in her short skirt and tight blouse she more clearly resembled the Marishka of the previous night.

We had a thick beef soup, bread, even butter and wine. We sat opposite each other on unstable rattan chairs. I apologized. She had done nothing wrong. I wasn't sure why I was so annoyed by her response to the film but if I felt nothing for my comrade Lucca, why should I feel anything about Charlie, the tramp? Her tears oppressed me, offended me, pushed me close to the outrage of weeping.

I mixed English with French, got tenses wrong. *"Pardon?"* she said, confused, but I pushed ahead and she seemed to catch on. *"Si, Si,"* she said, *"je comprends,"* and I moved my chair till we were next to each other and I put my arm around her and she leaned her head on my shoulder and we went to her room and undressed, lay in her bed and connected, and I don't know where it came from—it was uncalculated and without ground and completely surprised me. I said, "I love you"—I have no idea what I meant, I don't know what the feeling was that I named. I had no other name for it, a sudden release of the heart, a relief from the press of time—the war for a moment distant.

< 104 >

"I am content," I said, and she said, *"Moi, aussi."*

This was a long way from "love" but even "content" was too large a claim. I lay there, clinging to contentment and it slipped away. I was already back with my platoon, spinning the story of my leave, Marishka at its center, Red there, the Moulin Rouge, Paris, the supply complex at Esch. I had no idea who had survived the advance to the Rhine and who would be there to hear about my leave.

We were still in bed when Bernard pushed the beaded strings aside, arms spread wide against the frame of the entry, a dark, wiry, eagle-beaked Frenchman, perhaps in his mid-twenties. Annie was behind him, looking over his outspread arm.

"You bring your work home again?" he asked Marishka, barely glancing at me. "I thought we had an agreement."

"What agreement?"

"That this is not your place of business."

"Léo is a friend. He is a student."

"He comes to my home to study cunt?"

She said, "Fuck you, Bernard."

Before leaving, Bernard looked back at my uniform. He said in English, "This time she brings an American."

I got out of bed and dressed. "You said they wouldn't be home."

"This is my home, also."

She put on a negligee and followed me into the other room. They were at the table, wearing what looked like military discards. The tan army jackets were French, the pants GI fatigues. The boots looked like military issue.

< 105 >

Annie, almost Bernard's double, not so tall, wore no makeup except around her eyes.

Bernard said mockingly in English, "I regret if I have disturbed you, monsieur."

"You don't disturb me."

"I should be a more gracious host. After all, you have come to liberate our country. Perhaps you did not know my home is not in need of liberation."

"Tomorrow he returns to the war," Marishka said.

I hadn't come here to fight battles and didn't need him to be gracious. In any case, *Bonne nuit.*

Marishka walked me out into the hallway. "They told me they would be working all night."

No problem. I had to go anyway.

She asked, "You will write to me?"

"I will write to you."

She told me the address on the rue du Bac. I had nothing to write with, but was sure I'd remember. We embraced, kissed, and I was on my way back to the war.

< 106 >

❮ SONGS OF WAR ❯

There was good news on all fronts. The Allied armies were at the Rhine. The Luftwaffe was diminished and we had control of the air. The Russians, squeezing hard from the east, had crossed into Poland and were aimed toward Prussia and Berlin. The war in Europe would be over once we met the Russians.

I rejoined the company in a resort town on the west bank of the Rhine. It had been easy going all the way, no casualties. The medic who took my place wasn't needed. No one even remembered his name.

Worrying about the platoon had troubled my leave. I didn't know who would be dead or alive when I returned. I was afraid I'd have to join a morning assault as soon as I got back. But there was the company by the Rhine, disengaged and idling on a breezy, sunny day, waiting for a bridge to be repaired.

I gave Maurice all the details when he asked about Paris, even Marishka's "ooh la la" and how she looked on the bidet.

"Sounds terrific," he said. He liked the idea of a Sorbonne student hustling at the Moulin Rouge. He liked the idea that she surveyed the scene before choosing her clients. He liked the image of her sitting on the bidet in full view. He liked the faking of innocence. "Sounds like my kind of woman," he said.

I told him there was no faking. She was really a student. She roomed with other students, Bernard and Annie, in an apartment on the rue du Bac near the Seine. The hotel where she worked was called Hotel de l'Avenir, Hotel of the Future, and lying in her arms, I could imagine my future.

He listened carefully, then offered his verdict. "You're probably just one of a thousand, greener than most. My advice is, next time play it safe and use a rubber."

"Talking to you is a stupid idea. I don't know why I keep doing it."

"I'm kidding, Doc. The Future is a great name for a hotel. There's no better future than to be wrapped up in pussy."

I wrote Marishka, trying to stabilize a feeling that was ill defined to begin with and became something else as I talked about it. I couldn't remember the rue du Bac number and addressed the letter to Mlle. Marishka at the Hotel de l'Avenir. I had no last name and no street address and didn't know if there was any chance the letter would get to her. I told her I'd never forget our two days together and hoped she would also remember. I promised to look for her in Paris. At the end of the letter, I said, "I love you," knowing it couldn't be true, but the words generated the

< 108 >

feeling I wanted. I held the letter a couple of days, then decided if I had the nerve to face shell fire, it should be easy enough to make a fool of myself and I gave it to the mail clerk.

THERE WERE CHANGES in the platoon. Sergeant George, a gruff New Englander, had come from the Third Platoon to replace Lucca. He was a no-nonsense soldier, Captain Dillon's kind of man. There was a new squad leader, Corporal John Novak, a heavy-chinned farmer from Wisconsin: easygoing, likeable, slow to judgment. Novak knew about Lucca and the rockets. He told me if anyone deserved a leave it was me and he hoped I'd made the most of Paris.

I told him that when I came up from under Lucca I was in shock and nothing seemed real and it stayed that way until I met Marishka.

He said that a couple of good days in Pig Alley would cure anyone's troubles.

"It doesn't cure my big touble," I told him, "which is that I talk too much." I couldn't shut up about Marishka. I thought the feeling of joy would stay with me if I kept talking. We avoided talking about Lucca and he faded away.

TWO OTHER REPLACEMENTS came to the platoon while we idled at the Rhine. They were both named Jones, one called Roy, and the other Frank. Novak called them the Jones Brothers, an obvious joke since even at first meeting you could see they were polar opposites.

< 109 >

I warmed up to Frank Jones but it wasn't easy being with Roy. Roy was the skinny Louisiana kid I saw kill two German prisoners in a gully outside a German village. He came to us from the Second Platoon. He looked like a minister, spectacled and severe. Frank once called him a minister of death.

Roy had a surprising voice. When the clerk yelled, "Jones!" at mail call, he boomed a resonant, "Hyo!," his voice heftier than himself. Roy was avid for hometown news. There was always a bundle of mail for him. When he got hold of the *Bayou Sentinel* nothing could distract him.

"What you reading about, Roy?"

He was glad to let you know. We had plenty of time during that week by the Rhine. He was reading about ergot, a mold that infected dry oat grass and made sheep crazy. He was reading about a tomato blight that could ruin a crop overnight. There was more than farm news in the *Sentinel*. The hometown weekly mirrored Roy's faith, which was passed on to us in the form of his likes and dislikes.

Roy didn't like commies because they were against God and property. He didn't like Nigras from up North because they didn't know their place. He didn't like Krauts because they were the enemy. He didn't like the Japs because they were not only the enemy, but rabid. He didn't like the Frogs because they had sex like animals; didn't like the Limeys because they thought they were superior when in fact, said Roy, they weren't worth shit. He didn't like New Yorkers because they were out to fleece country boys and other good Americans. He especially didn't like

< 110 >

Frank, the other Jones, whom he suspected of being a Nigra-loving commie New Yorker.

He waited for you to react to his litany so he could determine if you were friend or foe. I should have been listed among those Roy Jones didn't like. We had nothing in common, neither music nor food nor racial attitudes, certainly not politics or religion, but Roy had decided that I was only Doc, an unarmed medic, above the fray, the same order of being as a judge or a preacher or a civilian or a woman, and, therefore, no competition. It was irrelevant to him that we were the same age and that I had no advantage in experience.

He liked Generals MacArthur, Patton, and MacAuliffe because they were tough as iron. He respected Captain Dillon and Lieutenant Klamm because they weren't bullshitters. He liked country people and other plain folks. He liked his state, his small town, and his Jones clan on one side and his Riley clan on the other. He got along with Maurice Sully because Maurice had a great voice.

In time I learned that Roy's loyalty to those he decided were friends was unconditional. He was ready to share his rations and loot, offer advice on how to deal with homesickness, sexual anxiety, and farm problems such as sheep intoxication and tomato blight. He was respectful when he spoke of women he considered decent. He regarded prostitutes as disposable property. You paid for her, she's yours, do what you want.

He entertained us with country wisdom and song, such as a country blues song he called the "Trifling Song," delivered lugubriously and accompanied by a twanged

< 111 >

guitar. It was about cheating women. "I wouldn't trust a one," the song says. "She'll trifle on you," and, "Lord, you'll nearly lose your mind." The only way to keep her from trifling was to "lock her up at night and watch her closely, too."

I asked Roy whether any woman had ever trifled with him.

"No one ever trifles on me, Doc. Ever."

Roy didn't allow any trifling and that meant, I think, he couldn't bear any challenge to his point of view. Anything alien to him was a threat he wouldn't permit.

If I hadn't seen what this skinny country boy could do when provoked I would have dismissed him as a fool. He defied good sense every time he opened his mouth. If you could feel superior to Roy you might find him merely ridiculous, you might ignore his goofy ideas and even see that in his odd way he could be good-hearted and generous. But I had seen Roy kill two German captives in a gully outside a German village within fifteen yards of me, and I wasn't inclined to take him lightly.

FRANK, THE OTHER JONES, was older than most of us. His dense mustache and burly frame gave him a buccaneer appearance. He had joined us late because his radical politics had made him an undesirable recruit. He was a veteran of the Spanish Civil War, presumed to be a member of the Communist Party. He had persisted in trying to volunteer for our war and was finally allowed to join —what he alone in our outfit called—"the war against fascism."

< 112 >

Frank Jones didn't get mail, because he was no letter writer. He left his Brooklyn home during the depression, still a kid. He never stayed at an address long enough to establish a base for correspondence.

In 1937 he volunteered to join the Spanish Loyalists. He was smuggled from France across the Pyrenees, given a uniform and weapon, sent, after one day's rifle instruction, into battle outside Madrid. He claimed that of the four hundred American recruits who fought at Jarama only eighty came through alive and uninjured and he was among the chosen.

When later we marched into a German village on the other side of the Rhine, Frank sang a song of the International Brigade in a German learned from his Brigade buddies. *"Die Heimat ist weit,"* he sang, concluding with an explosive, *"Freiheit!"*

Lieutenant Klamm asked Frank what he was singing. "An ode to freedom," Frank said, and translated, "Our homeland is far, yet we are prepared, to battle and conquer for you, Freedom!"

The lieutenant asked what homeland he was talking about.

"The homeland of freedom lovers."

"Get a different tune for this war, Jones. Why don't you try something like, 'Skinnamarinkydinkydoo'?"

Frank irritated me as my father sometimes irritated me. He declared himself when no one asked. He put himself center stage in an abrasive way before anyone had challenged him. The men might have accepted him despite his background. Once they got to know him they were ready

< 113 >

to discount his offbeat point of view. Frank didn't want to be discounted. He sang the Lincoln Brigade songs defiantly, as if he were in an enemy camp. The attitude was, this is what I believe and you don't, so fuck you.

He listened to the story of my Paris leave and it didn't trouble him that Marishka operated as a prostitute. He knew what it was to have to hustle in hard times. He was impressed with her generosity.

"Look for her when the war's over," he told me. "She sounds like one in a million."

It was exactly what I wanted to hear.

Roy hated the German songs. He said of Frank, "He's all talk and none of it's American." He asked Frank, "Whose army you in, anyway?"

"The army of free men, comrade."

"Don't call me 'comrade,' you Red fuck!"

"How about 'asshole' then?"

Roy mistook me for a friend and so didn't bayonet me when I squeezed between them.

Maurice had a far better voice than Frank's, and he countered the ode to freedom, with some verses of Casey Jones. The penultimate verse went:

> Ole Casey lined a hundred women up against
>   the wall
> Bet ten dollars he could frig 'em all
> Frigged ninety-nine and he had to stop
> 'Cause the friction on his pecker made his
>   balls red-hot.

< 114 >

I warned Frank that if he wanted to be around to see the end of fascism he'd better not light fires under Roy. There was no lid to restrain Roy once he started boiling over. I told Frank about the killings we'd witnessed.

Frank wasn't impressed. "I met shitheads like Roy before. He is not unique."

IT WAS ALMOST spring when we crossed the Rhine. The crossing turned out to be easy, nothing like the Sauer. Germany had disgorged all that it had swallowed of Europe. We had arrived in the German heartland and there were clear signs the war was near its end. The German prisoner of war, once exotic, was suddenly commonplace. A single GI, M1 slung over his shoulder, could march a company of docile, despondent PWs to the rear without worrying that any of them would try to escape. Where could they go? Behind us, their land was ours. Behind them, the vengeful Russians were coming. Hungry, dirty, tired, the Germans were now as accustomed to defeat as they once had been to victory. It gave us a different sense of German soldiers, whom we had once considered awesome predators—well clad, well armed, well disciplined, red in tooth and claw. Now they were flock animals, indistinguishable from each other. It was rare that we singled one out.

We did find one who clearly stood out while vainly trying to lose himself in a bedraggled squad of prisoners. He resembled a Hollywood version of a Nazi villain: tall, blond, blue-eyed, aloof. He had stripped himself of unit in-

< 115 >

signia but you could tell from his bearing and the quality of his clothes that he was an officer. He wore a braided overseas cap rather than a helmet. His gray jacket was tailored, his pant legs puffed out over burnished paratroop boots. His hands didn't shoot into the air when Lieutenant Klamm yelled, "Hands Up!" I translated in the same tone, *"Hände hoch!"* He slowly raised his hands chest high. He smirked when Roy patted him down, as though he knew the whole repertoire of intimidation and scorned our timid efforts. I say "our" because I felt the same outrage as the other GIs at his reluctance to acknowledge he had been defeated. He was what we feared and hated.

Lt. Klamm asked if he was SS.

He smiled, shrugged, said mockingly, *"Nicht verstehe."*

The Lieutenant told me to ask in German.

"Sind sie SS?"

He said he was a prisoner of war and would answer questions about his name, rank, serial number, nothing else. *"Gar nicht anders."*

"I don't give a fuck about his name, rank, or serial number. I want to know if he's SS."

"Ich muss nicht antworten."

"He says he doesn't have to answer."

"Tell him to take off his jacket. I want to see if he's got a tattoo."

He folded his arms, not about to take off his jacket. Roy, who was standing by, clicked off the safety of his rifle and leveled it at his chest. He shrugged, removed his jacket.

"He maybe don't understand your kraut," Roy said, "but he sure knows my M1."

< 116 >

"Now the shirt," the lieutenant ordered.

"Jetzt das Hemd."

"Was wollen sie?"

We wanted to see if he was SS. We wanted to know if he belonged to the crew that had slaughtered GI prisoners of war, wiped out the Czech city of Lidice and all its inhabitants, tried to empty Europe of its Jews.

He refused to take off his shirt.

The lieutenant said if the man didn't show him there was no tattoo he'd assume it was there.

"Okay," he confessed in British-tinged English, "I am with the *Schutzstaffel*. So what?"

He knew "so what." Why else was he trying to bury himself in the crowd? It wasn't till later that I imagined the fear behind his defiance. He knew what he would have done on the other side of the gun. He was doomed yet obliged by his discipline to preserve a façade. We would have found the tattooed insignia on his upper arm anyway.

The lieutenant left for a company briefing without, as far as I know, giving orders disposing of the prisoners. They were all marched to the rear except for the SS officer. Roy took charge of him. He prodded him into the woods with his rifle. We didn't hear any shots. A few minutes later Roy came out of the woods alone and raised his rifle high, exposing the bloody butt plate.

He'd stamped the man out, ruined his good looks and clean uniform, erased his sneers.

Frank said, "Maybe there got to be Roys. I just wish they stayed on the other side."

• • •

< 117 >

WE WERE OUT of practice at facing danger. We rarely advanced anymore on foot. We drove into towns in two-and-a-half-ton trucks, expecting German soldiers to be assembled for surrender. We were beginning to adjust to the idea that the war would be over sooner rather than later. Home was in the offing. We were out of rhythm with combat when we came to a small village and met camouflaged German tanks at the edge of town. There were two tanks and they cut loose with machine-gun fire. We groveled in the furrows of a plowed field in sight of the town. Not all of us groveled. Roy lay on his stomach in a furrow, deep into his hometown news. Dirt kicked up around him, and he kept reading, and I realized that alone among us, he lacked fear. Not that he'd overcome fear and reached a nobler condition, but that somehow his imagination wasn't large enough to provide ground for fear. That made him all the more intimidating.

The German resistance didn't last long. Artillery was called in and the tanks took off with the first barrage. Mortars dumped on the German trenches. White flags came out. We entered the town without suffering casualties. We called on the villagers to head toward the church, and strolled easily through the town. There was a rifle shot, and we scattered; the lieutenant yelled at us to get back in line and behave like veterans instead of green recruits.

We were pissed off at having been made to feel green, and when a scout found a shallow cave in a hillside at the edge of town where the shot might have come from, we let happen what happened.

Fisher, the light machine gunner, set up at the mouth of

< 118 >

the cave with his team. Someone inside yelled something I couldn't make out. Perhaps they were trying to surrender. Fisher was quick on the trigger and opened up and raked the cave and kept on firing and when it was over I found six dead German soldiers and one still alive, a bullet hole between the eyes. Fisher was nervous about what he'd done and wanted us all to be part of it. He called to me to come out of the cave. "Nothing you can do for him, Leo. He's finished."

I bent to the man and there was nothing I could do.

Fisher shouted again, "He's done for. Let's go."

"You go," I yelled. "I'll catch up."

Fisher waited outside while I huddled by the man and let him finish dying. We trotted to catch up with the platoon. We'd always been cordial. He came from Michigan. He seemed even younger than me, had only begun to shave, and maybe had something to prove. I wouldn't talk to him and he was no doubt relieved when we joined the others, who praised him for his nerve.

The mood was savage as we searched the town. Two German soldiers were rousted from hiding. Roy chased them into the cellar of a house followed by Hamilton and Alfieri. The Germans had dumped their weapons, obviously intending to surrender. Perhaps they fled because they guessed Roy's intent. Novak went into the cellar a few moments later. The Germans were folded on their sides, legs drawn toward their chests, blood on their throats and uniforms. Roy wiped his knife on one of the dead as if signing in as author of the scene. Hamilton and Alfieri did the same.

< 119 >

"That's how you treat hogs, not men," the Wisconsin farmer said later.

I had some baseless notion, grounded only in vanity, that if Roy considered me to be like a priest or judge or woman, someone above the fray, he might respect my moral authority and let himself be restrained. The fact is, he tolerated me only so long as I didn't get in his way. I could no more affect his actions than I could change the course of a twister.

I needled him but kept it light. "Hog butcher of the world," I called him.

"What?"

I recited the opening line of Sandburg's poem.

"Think you know something about hog killing?"

I said the poem wasn't really about killing hogs.

He described a hog killing, the snout wrenched back, the throat cut, the body hung and bled and slit, the guts pulled out. He mocked frail women who couldn't bear the squealing. Poor animal, his mother said when she saw him butcher the no-longer-productive family sow. But her grief didn't stop her from smoking the hams and rendering the fat. He turned my devious insult into another occasion to sneer at the hypocrisy of bleeding hearts. He placed me among the frail.

"Frailty, thy name is woman," I said.

"You said it," he said. "I didn't."

GERMANY—AT FIRST frozen and intractable—warmed, ripened, yielded its fruit, exposing more than we were meant to see.

< 120 >

In early April we came to a crossroads outside Kassel, an industrial city in the state of Hesse. One road led to the forest, the other to the center of town. The company officers met at the intersection to decide which road to take, and our platoon was detached, the rest of the company proceeding into Kassel without us.

Maurice had looked forward to Kassel. He'd heard that optical and precision instruments were manufactured there. He hoped for steals in quality binoculars. The lieutenant told him to forget it, "Kassel's not for you," and we took the road into the woods.

"What's in the woods?"

"Not binoculars."

The narrow road was hemmed in by cedars that strained the late afternoon light and dappled the asphalt. We couldn't see into the deeply shadowed forest but it was obviously well tended. Underbrush had been cleared away. Downed trees had been sawed into cord lengths then split and stacked in neat piles along the roadside. The lieutenant warned us to stay out of the woods. The road had been swept for mines, but the forest paths were still dangerous.

We arrived at a clearing, the forest cut back, three drab barracks tucked into the gash, the entire compound girdled with barbed wire. A master sergeant from headquarters was waiting in a jeep. Lieutenant Klamm went over to talk to him and returned with information about our post.

We had come to a *lager*—a camp—and in this *lager* there were thirty-five Hungarian women. Whistles and yelps, which he cut off with a wave of annoyance.

"These women have been through hell," the lieutenant

< 121 >

said, "some of them just kids. This morning is the first time they've seen American troops. They think we're their liberators. That's what they think now and that's what they're going to think when we pull out. So, no fraternizing. You can say, *Guten Tag,* but no screwing around."

He waved over Sergeant Solomon, perhaps in his mid-forties, tall, gaunt, wiry hair, slightly stooped, eyes bottomed with white, a swarthy, wrinkled face, something of a basset-hound look. He told us that the women were the only Jews from their Hungarian village still alive. They had been used as prostitutes for German troops garrisoned around Kassel. Our coming was to them a miracle. We had arrived just before the start of Passover, the holiday commemorating the liberation of Jews from slavery in Egypt. Food was being sent from the battalion, and the platoon was invited to observe the improvised seder meal. There would be a hot meal for us afterward.

He asked if there were any Jews in the platoon. Maurice said, "The aid man is a Jew."

"What's your name, Corporal?"

"Leo."

"Leo, you'll sit with me and the girls."

I told him I had never taken part in a traditional ceremony.

"No problem. Nothing's even kosher about this. We don't have the makings. The important thing is we're here with these girls to celebrate their liberation."

He called them girls as if what they'd suffered hadn't stripped them of girlhood.

I followed my platoon into the first barracks, a long

< 122 >

room filled with cots strung with rope webbing, a wood stove at the far end. We dumped our gear and sprawled on the bunks.

Frank Jones asked why I seemed reluctant to participate.

I told him I didn't know the ritual and felt awkward about participating.

"You heard what those girls been through. Shit, man, if you can take care of the dead and dying, you can sure take care of your own."

A truck arrived with sawhorses and planks and folding chairs, and we set up tables in a column almost the length of the middle barracks. A jeep brought hot food in metal urns and pots. We set the table with tin plates and canteen cups and mess-kit gear. We arranged stubby GI candles down the center of the tables. There were bottles of un-labeled German wine, white and red.

The women entered, shepherded by Solomon. They were dressed in gray shifts with three-quarter-length sleeves; their throats were bare, their hair cropped in rough spiky cuts. He led them to their seats. The men lined up around the table, against the walls. Solomon motioned me to sit next to him at the head of the table.

He spoke to the women in German. We were their lib-erators, soldiers of the American army, here to ensure their freedom and safety. He asked their names and they whis-pered, each in turn, hunched over, eyes downcast. The woman next to me was named Leona. She was prison pale, her black hair brutally cut. She had large eyes and full lips and a nice figure, and you could see why she had been saved for the use of the German soldiers.

< 123 >

I apologized to her for seeming awkward but I wasn't an observant Jew and was unfamiliar with the ceremony.

She said in English, "You speak German well."

"Nur ein bischen." Only a little. "Not as good as you speak English."

"I speak terrible. Forgive me, please."

"Nothing to forgive."

"We are very nervous. We cannot believe this is happening. We are almost dead."

She told me that in the morning the camp commandant had assembled the women and told them to say farewell to the *lager,* they were going to Kassel. First, he ordered them to strip. They were seated naked, their hair cut close to the scalp with big shears. They didn't have to worry about catching cold, the commandant told them. They were going to Kassel to be publicly executed. They were marched naked into Kassel, the first time they had entered the city. They came like sheep being led to market, but unlike sheep they knew that at the end of the journey they faced humiliation as well as death.

They were alive because their captors heard our guns and feared retribution. They were marched back to the *lager,* the doors locked, and it was our soldiers who next opened the doors.

Frank, standing behind me, heard it all, and passed on the information to the rest of the troops. He leaned over and assured her in his fluent German that we were their guardians. She was completely safe. He personally would see to it that she had nothing to fear. He said to Leona, "If

< 124 >

a tiger breaks into this room he will have to eat me first. He will have no appetite left for you."

She smiled. "There are some men here in Kassel who are so terrible, better the tigers."

"You have a beautiful smile," he said, and that broke her up. Her weeping started the others weeping. Solomon calmed them. Their troubles were over. They would suffer no more. They would see doctors and nurses and soon they would be on their way home.

"There is no one left," Leona said.

They would have new homes. If not in Hungary then in Palestine or the United States. He promised he would see that they reached safe haven. He had been given authority by the battalion commander to take care of our sisters.

He had improvised a seder plate in a makeshift service. He pointed to lettuce leaves meant to signify the bitter taste of exile and a bowl of crushed raisins and peanuts and honey representing the clay used in the labor of bondage. He uncovered a plate of matzos, sent by special messenger from division. The bread of our affliction, he said. A lamb shank bone stood for the paschal sacrifice. He said these materials were the best that could be managed. There was no horseradish, no hard-boiled egg, no parsley, but on this joyful night of the liberation of our sisters he declared the makeshift to be enough. He read from a mimeographed text, describing the order of service. He intoned a Hebrew prayer. He invited us all to drink wine. Wine was passed to the girls and to the GIs standing behind them. He gave me the mimeographed sheet and

< 125 >

asked me to read the questions, and I asked why this night of reclining and unleavened bread and twice-dipped bitter herbs differed from all other nights, and that led Solomon into a brief telling of the story of Exodus. He had a relaxed baritone voice, was a good storyteller, and it was a story everyone in the platoon knew. He spoke first in German for the girls, then in English. A few of the women timidly joined him in a Hebrew prayer. He asked us to fill our cups again from the wine on the table.

He managed somehow to forge a congregation. The forty GIs served the thirty-five women, lent their cups and mess kits, helped serve the food, stood against the wall, heads bowed while Solomon repeated the Hebrew prayer in English.

Afterward the singing began.

We sang "Go Down, Moses," not all the GIs joining in, but I could see a reverent Roy mouthing the words.

Maurice, with few biblical tunes in his repertoire, sang his King Solomon song. "King Solomon once, in his wisdom said, there's nothing quite like a good feather bed. . . ."

FRANK COULDN'T STOP talking about Leona in the days after we left Kassel. He felt the justice of our war was confirmed. We had uncovered pure evil and saved its victims. He said of Leona, What a beautiful woman. Think what she's been through, and still a sense of humor. That smile could break your heart. A truly beautiful woman, he said.

It wasn't a one-night fantasy. He was obsessed by Leona. He approached me as if she were a member of my

< 126 >

family and he could plead his case to me. She had suffered and survived. He couldn't forget her smile and her tears. He didn't want to let go of the experience of Kassel. He meant to keep track of her and find her. She was the woman for him.

"You're crazy," I said. He had a good heart but he was crazy. He'd been with her only a few hours, spoken to her only a few minutes, and now wanted to commit himself to her. That was pure fantasy.

"How about you and the girl in Paris?"

"That happened a hundred years ago."

WE PASSED THROUGH villages without getting off the trucks. We waved at villagers and drove on. We were three or four days out of Kassel and already beyond Hesse into Thuringia.

Frank pursued Leona with the same persistence that got him into the army. He cadged rides with the clerk Lovell to Battalion Headquarters. He met Solomon, who told him the women had been moved to a refugee camp near Kassel.

Lovell drove him to Battalion a few times. Frank told me he'd hit it off with Solomon. I think Frank could charm anyone if he put his mind to it. His enthusiasm could either light up a room or blow it up. He and Solomon were on the same wavelength, especially where Leona was concerned.

I was surprised that Frank got along with Lovell. Lovell was a conservative Southerner, reserved and cautious, a private man with no intimate connections in the company. He was a good clerk, stubborn but reasonable, who could

< 127 >

be cajoled into doing favors. On cold winter mornings we'd see Lovell at the assembly area before morning assaults. He brought mail and an urn of hot coffee. He wrapped his long, skinny frame in a wool greatcoat. He draped an olive drab scarf around head and face, the scarf secured by his steel helmet. As soon as we moved out he scooted back to headquarters, red-nosed and shivering.

Lovell and Frank weren't a natural fit. Lovell had a clerical temperament. His Southern roots were deep. Frank was rootless. He blew with the wind and the wind carried him sharp left.

He believed in a day, sure to come, when there would be no White, no Black, no Jew, no Gentile, no American, no German—all nations joined together in universal brotherhood, no longer divided by rank and privilege. That's what our war was really about, he said.

Most of the platoon thought Frank was all wet but after a few weeks they were used to him. They enjoyed his stories and ignored his politics.

Roy said, "He's a kook but there's a kook in every family."

ON EASTER SUNDAY, a couple of weeks after Kassel, we stopped at a village in Thuringia. We were on the road to Saxony. I was billeted with Novak's squad. An Easter feast was still warming in the kitchen of the house we took over. Eleven of us sat down to a meal of ham and wine and Easter pastries. Sergeant George and two other noncoms joined us.

Frank and Roy almost immediately started quarreling.

< 128 >

Frank had learned from Solomon that Leona was once again inside a barbed-wire enclosure, penned up with thousands of other refugees. It was no better than a prison camp with guard towers and armed MPs. He blamed General Patton. The refugee camps were in Patton's command, He treated the refugees like riffraff. Frank called him a two-gun asshole, a silk-scarf cowboy.

Patton was one of Roy's heroes. "How do you expect him to fuck around with housing when he's got a war to think about?"

Patton was one of Frank's villains. "What he thinks about is himself. He carries silver six-guns in twin holsters. He's a protofascist jerk-off with cowboy dreams of glory."

Roy said, "This Red fuck is spoiling my ham dinner."

"I hear the hog butcher talking," Frank said.

Roy was on his feet and Sergeant George ordered Frank to shut up and calm down. He was spoiling dinner for everyone.

Frank was jittery, almost manic, fueled by plundered German wine. Between his trips to Battalion and his platoon duty he wasn't getting much sleep. He went outside to smoke and calm down.

The Easter pastries were brought out. They were made of sweet pastry dough, covered with chocolate, crossed with white frosting. Private Alfieri, probably trying to lighten the mood, said, "I don't mind if white and dark mix in my Danish, just nowhere else."

I didn't want Alfieri to get away with what he'd just said. I usually kept my mouth shut but I had something to get off my chest. I was influenced by Frank's outspoken-

< 129 >

ness. These were my buddies, my platoon, and I felt iso-lated if I had to shut up about what I deeply felt.

"Speak up," Novak said.

"Does it matter to anyone if the guy next to you in your slit trench is white or black?"

They all agreed, even Roy, that in the heat of battle the ordinary rules didn't apply and you didn't see color.

"If Negro and White can get along in the worst of times, why not in the best of times?"

That was a minefield and no one wanted to go there. Race was woven into the fabric of American life. Pull on it and everything would come apart.

Frank, returning, heard what we were saying. He sat down and for a moment didn't speak. Then he started out calmly, trying to keep control, but he picked up steam and, of course, pissed off everyone.

He had once marched in a May Day parade. He carried a sign demanding freedom for the Scottsboro Boys. These were nine young black men falsely accused of raping a white woman in Alabama. They served life sentences. They had been sentenced, said Frank, by asshole bigots for a crime they never committed.

Alfieri asked, "What's a May Day parade?"

"A day celebrating the workers' revolution."

Roy said, "Then you are a Red."

"Better a Red than a fucking hog butcher."

Roy was out of his chair, smoldering, his face even more flushed.

Sergeant George told Roy to sit down, but he remained standing, considering bloody murder.

< 130 >

It was then that Lovell walked in, expecting a party. He'd come to visit his new buddy Frank. I was glad he'd come. He was Frank's pal and a Southerner. He'd never shown prejudice. No one had ever heard him say "nigger" or even "kraut." I hoped he would use calm reason to silence the bigots. I asked him as a Southerner and a reasonable, decent man, to answer a question. What did he think of Whites and Negroes being together?

"How do you mean together?"

"Serving together, eating together, living together."

Lovell said, "Pardon me. I don't want to get into this."

"Help us out. Everyone respects you."

He glanced at Frank but Frank didn't say a word.

After much urging Lovell reluctantly gave his opinion. It wasn't what I expected to hear. "Black and White are each right in their place. There's only trouble when they mix."

Roy nodded, "Okay!"

"What do you mean by 'mix'?" Frank quietly asked.

Roy said, "It's plain English if you know plain English."

Frank asked Lovell to tell him what he meant by "mix" in plain English or any other language.

Lovell gave an example. He was at a burlesque show in New York City. We were eager for a laugh to break the tension and the idea of a solemn, prissy Lovell looking up at a naked stripper was laughable and we guffawed. Roy told him to keep going and Lovell, more reluctantly, pressed on. "A Nigra was sitting in the front row. The stripper came out, and started to work and the Nigra stood up and yelled, 'Take it off!'" Lovell saw Frank's ferocious

< 131 >

glare and stopped. "I think I said enough. Maybe too much."

Frank asked mildly, "What exactly did you say? Check me if I heard you straight. You and a colored guy are sitting in a strip joint watching a naked white girl and he'd like to have sex with her just like you do. Is that what you said?"

A mournful Lovell said, "I don't make the rules, Frank. I live by them like everybody else. I'm not here to change the world."

"That's exactly what you're here for, to change the world."

Lovell repeated, "I just live by the rules like everybody else."

Frank bellowed, "You are changing the world, you damn fool. What do you think this fucking war's about?"

Lovell had remained standing and now turned to leave. Frank yelled after him, "You go to a burlesque show to jerk off and don't want some black guy to have the same pleasure!"

George told him to knock it off.

Roy said, "I thought I could get used to the son of a bitch but he won't keep his big mouth shut."

The dinner was broken up. Everyone left the table, except me and Novak and Frank. Novak wasn't part of the quarrel.

I walked out with Frank. "You lost a friend," I told him. "If you ever get mail now it won't be delivered."

Smartass, he called me. A worse case than the others. They, after all, didn't know any better. "Why don't you show some guts and take a stand for what you believe?"

< 132 >

FRANK WAS MISTAKEN if he imagined most GIs were out to change the world. If the world changed that's not what they meant to happen. They wanted the world to stay put. It was Germans and Russians who wanted to change the world. GIs wanted their service to pay off with gorgeous women, good jobs, more money, secure families, with nothing else changed. I say "they" but I mean me as well. I was part of "them" even when I didn't choose to be part of them. We all wanted to go home, everybody except Frank.

Like my father, he was another headstrong believer in the brotherhood of man, intolerant of any digression from what he considered to be the true path.

The trips to Battalion paid off for Frank. A couple of weeks after Kassel, he was transferred to Battalion Headquarters with the help of Sergeant Solomon. Frank meant Battalion to be the first stop on the trail of Leona. I don't know if he ever got closer.

I WROTE HOME about the seder at Kassel. I wanted to tell my folks that many of my buddies were goodhearted and generous. Some were bigots. A few were ignorant and cruel. But who, seeing the congregation forged by Solomon outside Kassel, wouldn't have hope?

Letters were censored at the company level and I was careful not to show myself in my letters. I wrote,

Dear Folks, We liberated thirty-five Hungarian Jewish women outside a German city. The Germans used them as whores. Our arrival saved their lives. My

< 133 >

buddies helped arrange a seder. It was led by an older man from headquarters named Solomon. I asked the Four Questions. I felt awkward and stupid but what we did was wonderful.

I received a letter from my dad some weeks later.

Dear Son, I gave up my faith when I was a boy because the pious Jews would not take arms in defense of our community. Now more than anything in this world it would have pleased me to be there with you to share that seder service with your comrades. For those poor girls I would again speak the old prayers and sing the old songs.

< 134 >

CHAPTER 8

< DISPLACED IN GROSSDORF >

In mid-April we entered Grossdorf, a village that the war appeared to have passed over. At its center was a market square, and around the square a small bank, a post office, a camera shop, a two-story hotel, a blacksmith, a hardware store, a butcher, a shoemaker, two or three cafés. The railroad station was a few blocks from the center. A seed warehouse was nearby. There was a textile factory alongside the mansion where we were quartered, not far from the town center.

The town was still in business. The bank had shut down but the post office still functioned. The shoemaker was still at work. There was an elderly barber still giving haircuts. The textile factory had operated until a few days before we arrived and was still intact and ready to start up. The camera shop was open. The railroad, of course, wasn't operating, but the depot restaurant still offered meals.

Agriculture was the main business of Grossdorf. Farmsteads were set right in town but market stalls were empty. The Wehrmacht had taken everything when it withdrew.

The village celebrated our coming. The citizens lined the main street and cheered as our truck convoy passed by. We had reached them before the Russians and they were now safe behind our lines.

I almost immediately discovered that Grossdorf had reason to fear the Russians, who were beyond Berlin and coming fast. Among the cheering citizens, there were some who didn't cheer. Shawled women with broad, Slavic faces stood off from the others. They seemed grim and forlorn. I asked one of the women where she was from. *"Wo ist dein heimat?"*

"Smolensk, in Russia."

She had fat, red cheeks, blue eyes. She looked solid and strong. She said that she and fifty other Russian women were penned up on the edge of town. There were Russian men at other camps. They had been brought here to replace Germans gone to war. She called herself, with bitter emphasis, a *Sklavenarbeiter,* a slave laborer.

After the Germans occupied Poland and much of Russia and the Ukraine, they abducted the Slav citizens by the tens of thousands and herded them into boxcars for transport to Germany. It was the Nazi intention to degrade the Slavs, reduce them to menials serving the Teutonic *Übermensch.*

Each dawn the women were released from the *lager* to do hard labor. They plowed, planted, hoed, raked, piled manure, drained cesspools into huge barrel wagons, swept the floors of the textile factory, cleaned the streets, were fed minimum rations.

They were now free but with no place to go. They

< 136 >

needed food and transport home. She begged me to help. *"Wir sind hungrig."* We are hungry.

I went to Lieutenant Klamm, who was busy setting up headquarters. We assumed our control of Grossdorf would last only until the arrival of Military Government with teams skilled in occupation duty. Till then our platoon ran Grossdorf.

I told the lieutenant about the camp of Russian women. He said to go ahead and check it out, he didn't need me around, but he warned me against any close contact with the women before they had been deloused. No touching or hugging or whatever else I had in mind. Typhus was epidemic among displaced persons, DPs, we called them.

The woman from Smolensk led me to her camp.

The town was flat save for a rise near its northern boundary. At the top of the rise I saw the drab barracks. I could smell the condition of the *lager* before I entered, a sharp odor, something foul countered by a strong disinfectant. Bunks were stacked to the ceiling. There was a latrine at one end and not much light.

I'm not sure how many women were inside — at least a couple dozen were in the shadows. More came in after me. They pressed around, touched my face and hair, murmured, *Chorny,* dark, as though darkness was a rare, treasured quality, their own fairness commonplace. They were all fair, some ash blond. Even dressed in bulky, cheap clothes, they seemed robust and handsome.

We communicated in a bare-bones German. Their mistakes with the language didn't coincide with mine and when I tried to speak of large notions such as slavery and

< 137 >

liberation they were confused. *"Was sagt er?"* What's he saying?

I said we had come to liberate them. They were no longer bound to their prison.

"Wir können heraus gehen? Wo sollen wir gehen?" We can leave? Where should we go? They wanted to know our plans for them. They had hardly eaten in two days and were desperate for food.

I explained that we hadn't known about the camp and so had no plans.

A blond woman with intense blue eyes pushed up front. Her dress was made from rough sacking material, but she was voluptuous with a regal bearing, obviously confident of how she would seem despite the poor dress and the dismal barracks. She put her hands on my shoulders, eye to eye, and commanded me to listen. "My name is Katrina. I, too, come from Smolensk."

She had a firm, strong voice. She spoke in a simple, less-than-basic German, the universal language of our war. She told me she was pregnant when taken from Russia. She was immediately assigned to a Grossdorf farm and set to work with hoe and rake and shovel. A daughter was born while she worked in the fields. The farmer wouldn't give her any time off. No work, no food. She became ill, her breasts dried up. The farmer refused to let her have milk for her baby and the baby died. A year had passed and she still waited for justice. Now the time had come. She wanted the slave master punished. *Jetzt.* Right now. No need for a trial. She wanted him hanged or shot.

What she told me deserved sympathy and I wanted to

< 138 >

sympathize but when she gripped my shoulders and pulled me close, I looked into her loose dress and saw her breasts and they didn't seem dry and empty. She smelled ripe and the smell gave me clues as to her strength and vigor. Perhaps she had no idea how she affected me being so close, and I tried not to look but I looked and she didn't pull away.

I said we would see to it that the farmer who employed her was punished.

"When?"

"I will take you to our officer."

Captain Dillon was at platoon headquarters and I introduced him to Katrina. "Katrina is a Russian, brought here to work in the fields. "

Captain Dillon was not an easy man. He'd been in action from Normandy on. He had a knack for sizing up a situation and taking strong action. He was an enormous improvement over our first company commander, the erratic Captain Roth, who gave up command after a slight wound. Dillon couldn't be conned or seduced. He studied Katrina, asked what language we used.

"German like everyone else."

"What's her problem?"

I asked Katrina to tell him about the farmer and her baby and you didn't need to know German to experience the intensity of her telling. I put her fervor into my translation and the captain said he wanted to see the camp.

The three of us entered his jeep and drove to the *lager* on the hill. Katrina preceded us into the barracks and announced in a loud voice, *"Ein Offizier kommt."*

< 139 >

The women swarmed around the captain. When would they be fed? When would they be returned home? When would justice be done?

He held up his hands to hold them off. "Tell them our Military Government will be here soon to answer all their questions."

Military Government consisted of teams of German-speaking GIs trained in the adminstration of conquered territories. They usually followed in our wake but hadn't kept up with the speed of our advance.

The first woman from Smolensk introduced herself as Anya and asked me to explain to the captain that they were starving right now. "We cannot wait. We must have something to eat."

"They're hungry," I told him. "They had nothing to eat today."

"They'll get something to eat. I'll personally see to it. Tell them that. Now let's go to where Katrina worked."

She sat up front in the jeep and directed us to a farm on the outskirts of town. Farmland encircled Grossdorf, spreading up the hillsides to the forests above. The farmhouses and barns were in town, set off the main street.

We drove into the enclosed farmyard through a wood slat gate. House and barn were side by side, manure heaped near the barn almost to the height of the barn doors.

The farmwife, a gaunt woman, gray hair pulled back in a knot, flinched at the sight of Katrina. Her husband was not here, she said. He was in the field working by himself. She would go find him. It would take only a minute.

< 140 >

"Tell her to stay put. We'll find the guy."

The farmer was in his field, hoeing furrows. A pungent, weedy fragrance was released from the newly turned soil. He broke up clots of earth, hacked weeds; he was a burly peasant, perhaps in his mid-fifties, somehow excused from war, unshaven, with a thick, dark mustache. He wore striped overalls, a shabby dirt-brown sweater, a cap with a bill. He looked up as we approached, then resumed working.

Yes, he remembered the woman. She had been in his employ. He didn't know about her baby. He denied having anything to do with the death of her child. He kept on hoeing, his manner curt and surly.

The captain said, "Tell him he has been chosen to feed the women of the *lager.*"

The farmer glared at me when I translated the captain's order. *"Unmöglich!"* Impossible. He had no food to give. *"Gar nichts. Alles kaput."* And resumed hoeing.

The captain unholstered his sidearm, placed the muzzle against the man's head, straightened him up.

"He will feed all the women every day. Beginning today. Tell him."

The farmer begged for understanding. *Bitte.* Please. War was terrible. It was a hard life for everyone. He lived no better than those who had worked for him. Whatever the woman had told us was not true. Everything was gone. His two sons had vanished at the Russian front. Horses had been taken away after the field was plowed. Now he labored with hoe and rake and shovel and scythe as it was done in ancient times. He worked alone with only his wife to help. Life was awful, not worth living. *Alles kaput.*

< 141 >

"Tell him I hold him responsible for bringing food to the *lager*. If he fails I will shoot him."

Where would he get food? The Wehrmacht had taken all stores in their retreat. There was nothing in Grossdorf. The officer might as well shoot him.

"Starting today and then every day, he will be responsible for feeding the women."

The farmer said all he could do was try.

I said to him, "Today and every day. Otherwise you will be shot."

Katrina said, "Shoot him now. He killed my baby."

The farmer said he would have to go to other farmers. It was their problem as much as his. He wasn't the only one to use foreign laborers.

"It must be done," I said.

"If the others give, I will give."

The captain said to tell the man he would check on what progress had been made. "I want the women fed by tonight. I hold him responsible. Tell him."

Katrina said again, "Shoot him now."

The captain dropped us off at platoon headquarters. He said to Katrina, "I will personally see to it you don't go hungry. You will get something to eat tonight even if we have to use company rations."

She wasn't appeased when I relayed the captain's assurance. Food wasn't her priority. She wanted the man shot.

I walked her toward the *lager* and stupidly put my arm around her waist and asked if she wanted to walk in the woods.

< 142 >

"What is in the woods?"

"You are beautiful. I would like to walk with you."

She shoved me away. She wasn't happy with the outcome. For months she had dreamed of justice and we had failed her. The farmer still lived. She was in no mood for a walk in the woods. "When you shoot the man, when you kill the murderer of my baby, then maybe I will walk with you in the woods."

"I am a medical person," I said, exaggerating my role so that she would understand it. "I do not kill men. I do not even carry a weapon."

"I need a soldier with a weapon," she said, "not a doctor. When our soldiers come—our Russian soldiers"—*unsere Kavaliere,* she called them—"then you will see justice."

I was disgusted with myself. More than once horniness had made a fool of me. My good intentions weakened when I looked down Katrina's blouse. I imagined how she had had to listen to her baby wailing day after day. She begged for food. There was no milk to spare for a slave-worker's baby. She wanted the man killed and she was right to want him killed. A peek down her blouse and I lost focus. I was young, brimming with appetite. In that candy shop of Grossdorf all goodies seemed available to the occupiers.

I returned to the *lager* the next day. The farmer had somehow found rations for the women and they were fed until the camp emptied a few days later. I met Anya in the town center once and asked where she was staying. "With my people," she said.

< 143 >

"And Katrina?"

She looked at me as if she could read my mind. "She is with us. We are waiting."

I understood her to mean they were waiting for Russian soldiers.

WE WERE HOUSED in the Schloss Hartmann, a massive three-story mansion with bared timbers and leaded windows and a mansard roof, a high-peaked tower above the porch. The outside timbers were painted black, the plastered walls a pale beige. It had been the residence of the owner of the textile factory next door.

All forty of us were billeted at the Schloss, two to a room. In my room there was a huge bed with a walnut headboard, capped with a crown finial, that was bent around like a ship's stern. The original linens were still in place, deep feather quilts inside floral slips. Dressers and bedside tables were marble topped.

The Schloss Hartmann deteriorated within days of our arrival. The quilts were messed, the marble stained, the floors scratched and scuffed. The burgomaster—the mayor—responding to the concerns of the owner, showed up with a crew of German women who restored order, though not to the original elegance.

Captain Dillon had instructed the burgomaster that until Military Government arrived Lieutenant Klamm would be the final authority over all town affairs. He would only intervene if security was at issue.

I was designated the unofficial translator.

The slight, elderly burgomaster, who knew a little

< 144 >

English, was entirely obliging. "My gracious sir, tell me what you wish and we shall cooperate to the fullest." He listened to my German, heard its limitations, and, without condescension—with the greatest humility—reduced his language to simple, clear sentences, embellished with English even more awkward than my German.

We discarded long johns and sweaters and walked Grossdorf in open-throated wool olive drab shirts, carelessly bearing weapons. There was little discipline. A desultory morning roll call, halfhearted calisthenics. I walked the cobblestone streets of a village that still maintained its ancient habits of deference, my sleeves rolled, helmet tilted back, the spring sun glittering in shop windows. The townsfolk bowed to me. Fräuleins smiled, offered curtsies, giggled.

The forests were dense, the grass high in the meadows, the air sexy. The fräuleins worked bare legged and wore loose blouses. Their men were gone, either at the Russian front or cordoned off in vast pens behind our lines. Elderly farmers worked the fields with their wives and daughters, scythe and shovel, rake and hoe. There were few tractors or horses or mules. Foreign labor was no longer available.

We called to the fräuleins when they returned from the fields, flushed and sweaty, shepherded by their fathers. Some managed to get GI messages despite the language problem and joined GIs in evening trysts at the Grossdorf cemetery or in the forest meadows above the town.

There was much available but I didn't know how transactions were to be made. One afternoon I met Ingrid Schultz, dressed in black, full figured, perhaps in her early

< 145 >

thirties. She walked down the street, lugging a heavy suit-case in each hand. She had a fine posture, wore her fair hair tied back, and was carefully made up as if she had come from important business. She was no peasant. I asked if she needed help with her luggage. She was star-tled, didn't understand. When I reached for a suitcase, she must have thought I was after loot and pulled away. I explained carefully that I only wanted to help and she cau-tiously yielded a suitcase. I introduced myself and apolo-gized for my poor German. I asked her name.

"Frau Ingrid Schultz."

"I would like to see you again, Ingrid."

She shrugged as if she didn't understand and flashed her wedding ring.

WE SETTLED DOWN to the easy rhythm of occupa-tion while waiting for the Russian army to reach us.

The DPs were also waiting. They gathered outside the farms where they had worked and stared at their onetime masters, who gave the former slaves wide berth. Justice, if it ever came to Grossdorf, promised to be brutal. Until that happened our days remained lax and carefree.

Part of the platoon was on guard duty at the Grossdorf border. Those not on duty looked for booze and food and loot, and flirted with the fräuleins. There was softball in a nearby meadow after lunch. You could hike in the woods. Grossdorf wasn't one of those tidy, neat, ancient villages huddled around a Gothic cathedral. It was more like a sprawling Iowa or Nebraska town. The architecture was ordinary, wood and plaster farmhouses with adjoining

< 146 >

barns. There were no cathedrals, just the kind of simple church you might see in the Midwest.

Our mansion was one of the more elegant places in Grossdorf, set deep in its lot next to the textile factory. The porch faced a vast lawn carved by a circular drive. We hung out on the porch after retreat, drinking Pilsner beer.

There was still guard duty, but most other details were taken over by DPs. They ran our kitchen, handled the garbage, cleaned our quarters, did our laundry. For compensation they received cigarettes and the excess of our meals.

The only sound of war was occasional rifle fire from GIs on guard at the city border, shooting at deer and birds and once at a stray cow. When the burgomaster timidly complained, the lieutenant ordered the shooting to stop.

Mail had caught up with us—magazines, newspapers from home. We wrote to family and buddies and sweethearts, our attention turning to life after war. In Grossdorf we improvised a strange peace before the war's official end. It was a peace with broken German as its lingua franca and American cigarettes the medium of exchange.

We had no clear idea as to how to conduct this quasi peace. Military Government was supposed to arrive with a plan for the occupation of Grossdorf. Until then we had little to do with running the town. We were privileged and powerful guests. Our main job was waiting for the Russian army. When it reached us the war would be over.

ONE AFTERNOON A young Dutchman came to our quarters to do business. He gave his name as Willy

< 147 >

Vanderzee. He seemed young for his age, nineteen or twenty, fair-haired, blue-eyed, almost pretty, neatly dressed, no apparent evidence of hard labor. You didn't see civilian men that age in Grossdorf unless they were DPs. He spoke an accented, but colloquial, English. He had picked up GI slang. He told us he was Dutch and had been pressed into German service as a textile worker and translator.

Roy Jones was suspicious of this too-well-off young man. "How do we know you're Dutch? You look kraut to me."

"Obviously I am not German. A German my age would be at the front."

"Show us your ID."

There was nothing soft about Willy, despite appearances. No show of subservience to win our favor, no smiles, no effort to justify who or what he was, no explanations, no apologies. Instead of an ID he flashed a roll of dollars and offered to buy our rations of PX cigarettes at twenty dollars a carton.

Maurice said, "Twenty bucks is ID enough. Let the kid be whatever he says he is."

That first afternoon Willy handed out two hundred dollars for ten cartons of cigarettes. It was a surprising bankroll. Dollars weren't easy to get. We were issued the occupation currency. The Germans didn't trust our version of their money and there was little the military mark could buy. Cigarettes and dollars were the accepted currency.

Willy's trade wasn't confined to cigarettes. "I am your man for whatever you need."

< 148 >

I asked if he knew the penalty for doing black-market business.

"Corporal," he said, in a cool, calm tenor, "I do not give a fuck."

Two days later Lieutenant Klamm found him inside our quarters and demanded an ID. Willy produced two cards, one official and one that he'd kept hidden. The official German ID, issued to foreign workers, named him Willem Vanderzee, nineteen years old, from the Netherlands, a language specialist and loom operator. The other card, Dutch, in poor condition, dated a few years earlier, displayed a photo of a sullen, sixteen-year-old Willem Frucht, *Jood* stamped in the center. Lieutenant Klamm asked what *"Jood"* meant.

"It means I am a Jewboy, sir."

"Well, which Willem are you?"

"Whichever one you like."

He'd kept the second card at the peril of his life and it was Willem Frucht he chose for his identity.

Willy spoke French, German, Russian, some Polish, in addition to English, and, of course, Dutch. His Russian and Polish had been developed during his year's service in Saxony, interpreting for the foreign workers. The other languages he'd picked up in good Dutch schools.

The lieutenant asked why he didn't return to the Netherlands.

"There is nothing for me there."

"You got no folks?"

"My future is here."

< 149 >

"What's for you here?"

He knew the politics of Grossdorf. He could tell us who we were dealing with. More important he could get us almost anything we wanted.

"With a little something for yourself?"

"Something for myself, naturally."

"What I've been looking for," the lieutenant said, "is one of those high-quality ceremonial blades, a sword or bayonet or a top-of-the-line hunting knife—high-grade steel with a great-looking inscription, you know, the Reich eagle etched over Gothic lettering."

"I can easily get that for you."

"And top-of-the-line Zeitz field binoculars."

"No problem."

"A Leica with wide-angle lens."

"The Leica is more difficult. I will see what I can do."

Willy quickly found camera and binoculars. The transaction cost the lieutenant several weeks of cigarette rations. It was the blade Willy couldn't immediately produce. He brought disappointing specimens that the lieutenant rejected. Willy said, "No problem. I will keep looking." While he looked, the lieutenant let him hang around our headquarters.

I ASKED WILLY why he had come to Germany.

"To save my neck."

He offered no details, almost vehemently refusing to disclose his personal history.

"The past is gone. Entirely erased. All questions are stupid because there are no answers. Everything begins now."

< 150 >

I was immediately attracted by his intelligence and nerve. Whatever he had experienced must have been enormous. A wartime journey from the Netherlands to the heart of Saxony by a Dutch Jew was beyond anything I could have managed.

We sat on our porch in the evening, apart from the others. It wasn't difficult to open up to Willy. It was a pleasure being probed by someone of his intelligence. I told him I was also Jewish and he nodded, no surprise. I told him about Lucca and Paris and Marishka and other stories of war.

He asked me one evening, "The war in Europe will be over, sooner or later. What will you do then, Leo?"

"There's talk of our being sent to the Pacific and fighting the Japanese."

"And after the Japanese?"

I had no plans beyond returning to Detroit and college. He pressed me about Detroit. I told him about my neighborhood, the main library, the art museum, the downtown theaters, Ford, the great factory at River Rouge.

"How will you earn a living?"

"Something will turn up. Anyway, my life will be at the college."

"What life is that?"

"The life of the mind, not commerce."

"Oh, yes," he said, "the life of the mind. I recall." He said mockingly that he had been a voyager in the land of the learned but wanted no credit for what he had learned. He recited the partial itinerary of a precocious schoolboy's journey. Before he had finished high school, he had read

< 151 >

some Shakespeare in English, much of the first volume of Faust in German, Corneille and Racine in French, stuff he would never read again. It was all without survival value, irrelevant to the business of getting on. He claimed to have stripped to the bone, no superfluous weight. "The life of the mind," he said, "is so much *dreck,* shit."

I told him I was not concerned with survival.

He said, "Then you will not survive." He called my attitude immature and stupid, especially for a Jew. "I listen to your story of war and think you must have learned something and yet here you are in Grossdorf, deep in the asshole of Germany, still believing in the life of the mind."

"Yes," I said, "even here in Grossdorf."

He got up to leave. "This is one of the last things I picked up in my advanced German literature class. Georg Büchner wrote, a hundred and nineteen years ago, *'Lass uns nach Kreuz pissen, dahin ein Jüde stirbt.'* Let's piss on the cross—a Jew's dying there. After reading Büchner, what is there to say? Fuck the life of the mind, better commerce. A few dollars in your pocket, a few cartons of cigarettes in your pack, then, perhaps, you have a chance."

The war had turned this Dutch boy rock hard. There was no limit to his zeal for commerce. He disappeared for two or three days at a time, in disregard of curfews, somehow able to roam Saxony without benefit of passwords or passes. He showed up at our headquarters, loaded with dollars, looking for cigarettes, soap, chocolate, chewing gum, even toilet paper—whatever rations we carried. He had a precise cigarette and dollar equivalent for each bartered item.

< 152 >

He showed me parts of Grossdorf I wouldn't otherwise have seen. One day he saw me wave to Frau Schultz, coming from the textile factory. She smiled, waved back.

"You like her?" Willy asked.

I shrugged.

"You wish to meet her?"

"It's something you can arrange?"

"There is nothing easier. I know her well."

One afternoon he led me to a house behind the market where Ingrid Schultz lived with her two small children.

"She works when there is work at the textile factory. A widow for more than three years. She is past mourning and ripe for romance. She likes you, Leo. She waits for you."

They had been coworkers in the textile factory office. He had listened to her story of grief, consoled her with difficult-to-obtain bath soaps and shampoo, brought gifts of chocolate and chewing gum for the children. She had reason to be grateful.

Willy came in with me. She was waiting in what I presume were her best clothes, a velvetlike dark red dress, low at the bodice, breasts pressed up and braced. The blinds were down, the children gone. She only spoke German and her nervousness made it difficult for us to communicate. Yes, she said, she had met Willy at the factory, a *Wunderkind, das zahme Tier der Meisterin.*

"What's that?" I asked Willy.

"She tells you I was the boss's tame animal, her pet."

"You were her pet?"

"I was to her whatever was necessary."

< 153 >

Willy went to the kitchen which he obviously knew, brought out shot glasses and plum brandy, toasted our health, *"Auf ihre Gesunderheit!"*

He told me to walk him to the door. He whispered, "Four packs of cigarettes, and if you have them, one or two D-ration chocolate bars for the children. That will be sufficient."

She had overprepared, too much powder, the scent going stale after a little action. She was an attractive, thin-lipped, large-nosed woman, tightly bound at the waist and bosom, light hair coiled above her ears. She smiled stiffly. Her throat needed clearing. She asked if I wanted another drink. We sat on her couch, the door to the bedroom open, the bed visible. I could see lace pillow slips.

She said Willy was a friend, a remarkable person, but sometimes confusing. She had never regarded him as one of the foreign workers.

How was he different from the others?

She had never known anyone so young and yet so clever. He seemed entirely German.

We continued drinking. I sympathized with her nervousness, wanted to leave, but the only way out seemed to be through the bedroom, and we gave up the effort to talk, groped clumsily, her hair coming undone. I fumbled her red dress open. I struggled with corset and brassiere. I smelled her sweaty nervousness and the scent took me almost entirely out of the mood, but it somehow got done. I sought quick release, there on the couch, not on the bed. Afterward she offered me food and drink but I excused myself. I was needed at headquarters.

< 154 >

She was more attractive uncorseted and no longer trying. When she let go of the fixed smile, her face lapsed into sorrow. I left cigarettes and chocolate on the antique dropleaf table in the vestibule.

I reported to Willy that the pleasure was limited. The connection I had made with Marishka didn't happen with Frau Schultz. My impulse was to offer solace, not love.

"Neither solace nor love are called for in this transaction," Willy said. "Cigarettes and chocolate are sufficient."

To Willy everything was quid pro quo, or at least that's how he seemed to want it to be, cigarettes for dollars, sex for cigarettes, a momentary affirmation of existence for sex.

He was the man Maurice was looking for.

MAURICE'S STOOGE, NAGY, had carried a rucksack full of apparently worthless deutsche marks through much of Germany. Maurice offered Willy a percentage of the face value if he could dispose of the marks.

"You mean that as a serious offer?"

"Ten percent of whatever you get."

"You offer me ten percent of shit, my friend. That paper is junk."

But Willy figured out how the old marks could have some value and returned with a plan. The Germans didn't trust the occupation currency. If you knew where to look you could find businesses—not necessarily legal—where the old deutsche mark was still used and unwanted occupation marks had accumulated from GI trade. Willy knew where to look and could turn old marks into new, at a steep discount, of course.

< 155 >

The problem with the new currency was that GIs were limited in the amount they were allowed to convert to dollars.

Willy's plan was to use the military marks to buy U.S. postage. The stamps could then be exchanged for dollars without limit.

"You want me to buy stamps?"

Willy explained again—exchange the old marks for new, then use the new marks to buy stamps. That wouldn't be simple. The stamps had to be purchased in relatively small lots so as not to alert authorities. It required traveling to post offices throughout Saxony, buying here and there, representing themselves as collectors if necessary. Army post offices were open between nine and seventeen hundred hours on weekdays, nine and twelve Saturdays. They would need transportation, an area-wide pass, a number of IDs.

Maurice said he could arrange for passes and transportation and IDs, but how would they get dollars for the stamps?

"We will offer the stamps at a discount," Willy said. "No problem." He wanted 50 percent of whatever the stamps brought in and Maurice said, "The hell with it. Go ahead." Whatever could be exchanged for the outdated currency was so much gravy.

Willy wanted me involved but I refused to have any part in it. There were severe penalties for dealing in marks.

Willy said, "The first law of self-improvement is, you do not get rich sitting on your ass. I take it on myself—out of the goodness of my heart—to return you to Detroit a rich man."

< 156 >

I said, "No thanks. My buddies didn't die so I could hustle marks in Grossdorf."

Willy treated me as though I were the one displaced. "You will return to Detroit with your stories of war and roll around in the life of the mind and you will have learned absolutely nothing. I offer you, entirely without cost, a few valuable lessons."

"What's your interest?"

"You are a fool and a Jew, so"—he said mockingly in Yiddish—*"ich hob rachmoniss,* I take pity."

For someone so young and so displaced he was annoyingly cocksure.

THE SCHEME CAME off without my help.

Maurice secured transport and passes. He and Willy traveled each day, sometimes in the morning, sometimes in the afternoon. They traveled across Saxony along routes Willy had explored as freely as if the war were over. In a couple of weeks they disposed of the cache of apparently worthless marks and converted them to stamps.

Maurice complained afterward that the stamps were so deeply discounted he had ended up with little more than a hundred dollars. It was better than nothing but he was suspicious of the accounting.

Willy pretended to be shocked. "I thought you would thank me for turning nothing into something."

"Something for you, almost nothing for me." Still Maurice appreciated the buccaneer spirit. He told me, admiringly, "Be careful when you deal with the kid. Like me, he don't give a fuck."

< 157 >

Willy handed me twenty dollars. "For your part."

I had no part and didn't want his money.

"In Münden it seems you signed the postal receipt. The money is for the loan of your name."

I refused the money. I hadn't rented out my name. It was stolen from me. He knew I opposed his schemes. Why did he want me involved? Was he afraid I'd report him to the MPs? Then he shouldn't have let me in on the plan in the first place. I told him to watch out. He was a displaced person. He didn't belong here. His days in Grossdorf were numbered. Did he have no shame?

"What shame do you want me to have?"

"You encourage the stereotype of the Jew as a money hustler."

"I'll tell you in three languages what I think about that. *I do not give a fuck. I do not give a fuck. I do not give a fuck.*" By the third repetition he was snarling.

WILLY WAS POPULAR with the GIs. He knew our pleasure and aimed to please. He provided drinks and snacks for a weekly show Maurice put on at a saloon in downtown Grossdorf. Willy brought in a local accordionist, fiddler, and drummer to back Maurice's harmonica and singing. Willy was a source for our Pilsner beer. He crossed the Czech border to buy kegs of the light brew. He was able to pass behind Russian lines. We may have been immobilized waiting for the Russians, but not Willy.

Maurice put on his show on Friday nights, a program mostly of pop tunes, like "Oh, What a Beautiful Morning,"

< 158 >

"Amapola," "Green Eyes," "Paper Doll," "Frenesi," tunes the local talent could handle.

Maurice got us all singing, even Willy, who, one night in an almost toneless but heartfelt tenor, released a German version of *"J'attendrai"* to accordion accompaniment, the song I'd first heard at the Moulin Rouge.

Komme zurück. Come back, I'm waiting day and night for you, come back.

I had no idea whom this entirely self-sufficient Dutch boy could be waiting for.

Maurice quickly restored the party mood after Willy's sad song. "Enough kraut. Let's hear something in the imperial *Sprach,*" and he started playing "The Music Goes 'round and 'round."

The elderly German musicians floundered and Maurice shouted, *"Halte!"* and stopped them. He and his harmonica led us on.

MAURICE HAD SO LONG advertised his imminent departure that we no longer believed it would happen and it was a surprise when Special Services finally called. They wanted him for an army musical being rehearsed in Zwickau to possibly tour the Third Army theater of operations. He was to be immediately detached from the company and sent to Division Special Services.

Nagy told Maurice it would be no fun with him gone. "You weren't good for much but you were good for laughs."

The machine gunner, Fisher, urged him to take Nagy

< 159 >

along when he left. "We don't want to hear the dog howl when his master's away."

Maurice said he would take a Paris leave before joining the new outfit. "Want me to take a message to your girl in Paris, Doc? What was her name again?"

I hated the foxy grin, the redness of him, a slash of mustache, the flaming hair that perfectly suggested appetites on fire. He was hardly likely to defer to a buddy. It was the fault of my callow, brimming heart that he had learned the glories of Marishka. "I don't remember."

"It was Russian. Marishka something."

"She didn't have a last name."

"What was the hotel?"

I refused to recall.

"Something to do with the future?"

"You'll never find her there."

"What do you want me to tell her if I find her?"

"Tell her the messenger has lymphogranuloma inguinale, blue balls for short, and to avoid him like the plague."

Maurice left by jeep in the morning. I admired his nerve and zest and wished I could have his ease of action. But he only served himself, and that I never liked. I was depressed by the possibility that he might find Marishka.

< 160 >

CHAPTER 9

< THE FACTORY >

The textile factory was next to the Schloss Hartmann, separated from us by a wide lawn and a fence and a gravel
driveway. It was a one-story plastered concrete brick building that extended from the street to the block behind us,
the same beige color as our mansion. From the side porch
we could see looms and cutting tables and shelves of material through barred windows. The factory was inopera-
tive save for a few maintenance workers and the owner,
Fräulein Hartmann, who showed up every day and walked
past us, ignoring our close inspection.

She was a slim, broad-shouldered woman, in her early
thirties, always dressed in a long-sleeved white blouse and
black skirt, black walking shoes and dark stockings. She
seemed imperious and aloof, an attitude perhaps designed
to keep us away.

Her first task on arriving at the factory grounds was a
menial one. She filled a long-spouted water can from a
hose connection on the side of the building and watered
the rows of lettuce set among flowers that bordered the

factory side of the fence. It was so practiced an act I guessed she wasn't merely doing the chore because of a labor shortage.

She never raised her eyes from her garden to look at the house where she had lived and where we were now billeted. There was a rust-colored ceramic panel set above the porch entrance that bore her family name in Gothic lettering. SCHLOSS HARTMANN. *Schloss* means "castle" or "manor" and the house was no doubt the most impressive in Grossdorf, but naming it *"Schloss"* exaggerated its elegance.

The fräulein couldn't help knowing she was being watched, but she gave no sign she was aware of us. She didn't shrink from our scrutiny or rush her pace when she heard Roy Jones whistle.

Her dark blond hair was cut on the bias to the base of her head, exposing a long, firm neck. She had a strong chin, a good hunk of nose—no obvious beauty, but with her shoulders squared, her focus straight ahead, she seemed regal and superior and very attractive. Looking at it from the point of view of the two or three hecklers, her attitude flaunted the true state of affairs. Her garden belonged to us, Germany belonged to us, she and every citizen of Grossdorf belonged to us. Yet here she was, well dressed, apparently well fed, walking her grounds as if nothing had changed. Up the hill, the DPs, some of whom we later learned had worked in her factory, still had found no justice. And there could be no justice till the coming of Military Government. Roy Jones didn't care to wait.

When the fräulein passed by with her watering can, Roy yelled from the porch, "Hey, Fraulein High and Mighty,

< 162 >

me, Roy Jones, is waiting for you in the master bedroom to say, *Guten Tag.*"

I warned him—jokingly—that the fräulein was officer material.

"What does that mean?"

"It means she isn't available for enlisted men."

"Who asked you?"

"Just for your information."

The following morning he was waiting down by the fence when she arrived. She disregarded his *Guten Tag* and started watering. He followed along on our side of the fence.

"Let me introduce myself, Fräulein. My name is Roy Jones. I'm staying right now in what was your bedroom and I'm having a ball. Donkey shown. Let me return the favor with some advice about your garden. A big freeze is gonna get your lettuce."

She straightened up, continued watering, and he followed along.

"And if it ain't a big freeze it'll be something else. Fräulein, this garden ain't meant to grow. It's the gardener that's the problem. Good men died because of you."

She walked as if he weren't there, dunking her spout into the lettuce.

"Take my advice and don't waste time on your goddamn garden. It ain't going to make it. I promise you, Babe. *It's done for. The big freeze is coming. It ain't going to make it.*"

They walked out of earshot to the end of the flower border. Did he tell her about shooting German prisoners,

< 163 >

stamping out the SS officer with the butt of his rifle, bay-
oneting fleeing German soldiers? Did he impress on her
that he wasn't a man to be ignored? She entered the factory without a glance of acknowledgment.

I told Roy not to bother trying to educate this woman.
She probably didn't understand English.

"She understands all right."

"When the Russkies come they'll make her sing a different tune."

"I don't need Russkies to teach her what to sing. She'll
sing 'Dixie' before I'm through."

I kept my tone light and amused, close to mockery, but
sufficiently ambiguous so he wouldn't be too pissed off. I
didn't have the nerve to say, "You scare me, Roy. They
ought to lock you in the stockade and throw away the key
for everyone's peace of mind." He considered me, if not a
friend, then someone to be accepted.

Late one night we were awakened by howling. Roy, in
his fatigues, lit by moonlight, marched through the vegetables and flowers, goose-stepping, letting loose what
passed for rebel yells.

The lieutenant came out barefoot, wearing only khaki
shorts. "What the hell you doing!"

"Tending the bitch's garden."

"Haul your drunken ass out of there."

Roy, in no hurry, climbed back over the fence.

The lieutenant told Sergeant George, "I want the whole
platoon—everyone not on guard duty—assembled at oh-
six hundred hours. We're going to shape up before this
whole outfit gets busted."

< 164 >

In the early morning light we saw the damage. The lettuce was squashed. There wasn't a flower left standing. The rows of daffodils and tulips and irises were trampled flat.

The lieutenant called us to attention and put us at ease before he would have been obliged to challenge our slovenly coming to attention. He spoke in a shout. The war wasn't over. We still lived under military law. What had happened last night was unacceptable. We weren't here to destroy Grossdorf. We weren't Russkie barbarians. He ordered all drinking on the front porch of the Schloss Hartmann to cease. The beer keg would be removed. He was going to reinstitute a formal retreat and morning roll call.

We were still assembled on the front lawn, going through the charade of calisthenics, when Fräulein Hartmann arrived. She saw the ruined garden, did an about-face, and left.

She had coddled that garden, the first daily act of maintenance she performed in the regulation of her empire.

The burgomaster came on the run. *"Eine Schande,"* he said to me, nodding at the flowers. A shame.

I agreed. *"Eine Schande."*

"Dein Offizier, bitte?"

He spent time with the lieutenant, who understood enough of the burgomaster's English to do without a translator, and called Roy into his office and commanded him in a shout we all heard to apologize to the fräulein for destroying her garden.

"Hell no!"

"Hell yes, you mean!"

< 165 >

"The lady worked slaves in her factory. What's the big deal about lettuce and flowers?" Did she think a garden balanced her sins? She was lucky it was only the garden he'd trampled. What were a few rows of flowers when we'd flattened German villages from the Sauer to the Czech border? He'd heard there wasn't a block of Munich standing and Nuremberg was left with no identifiable address. The dead were so ordinary we passed heaps of them without noticing. "What the fuck use are flowers, anyway?"

The lieutenant warned him for his own good to stay away from the fräulein.

Willy, at the Schloss buying rations, overheard the quarrel. He was all for Roy Jones. He had small regard for the ruined garden. "She feeds her flowers better than she fed her DPs. Some of the women you met in the *lager* on the hill worked for the fräulein."

Willy himself had started out at the factory as a stock boy. He was elevated to the office staff to translate instructions to a polyglot labor force of Germans, Russians, Polish, a few French, and Dutch.

I asked how well he knew her.

"I would see her every day at the plant and here at the *Schloss*."

"What is she like?"

"If they had royalty in Grossdorf, Gretchen Hartmann would be the queen."

The factory was a family business and among the Hartmanns she was more the master than any other, Willy told me. She successfully managed in hard times. When more important factories in nearby Chemnitz were shut down

< 166 >

for lack of supply, she kept her plant going. When Allied bombing brought almost all commerce in Saxony to a halt, her Grossdorf plant was still operating. Of course, the output was army clothing—everything from winter underwear to overcoats—so the plant was especially favored by the Wehrmacht. Still, to keep it running she had not only to be very clever but concentrated and ruthless.

"When you speak about her you make her sound extraordinary."

"I have no sympathy for the extraordinary."

THE LIEUTENANT EVIDENTLY took some heat over the garden incident. The fräulein had friends. He gathered us again to discuss the garden incident. This time his manner was earnest and confidential. He said he wanted to talk buddy to buddy. Forget rank. We had survived the hard tests of combat together, buddies forever. When the war was over and we were back home sitting around the kitchen table, we'd tell stories about Irrel and Trier and the Siegfried line and the pillboxes and the villages and marching fire and realize that part of us would always be with the First Platoon. But we still had a mission in Grossdorf. We were responsible for its well-being. The burgomaster had told him that the factory was the largest employer in Grossdorf. The town's eventual recovery depended on the factory. "I know it's confusing," he said. Germans were the enemy. The nonfraternization policy was meant to keep soldier and civilian apart. But that policy had to be balanced against our need to be in communication with the civilians who governed the town. "If

< 167 >

anyone has a problem with the people next door, you come to me. I'm the one will deal with the problem. No one crosses that fence without my permission."

He asked me to stay after the platoon was dismissed. He wanted me to take a message to the fräulein apologizing for the damage to the garden, inviting her to the *Schloss* to discuss amends. "Tell her this evening, eighteen-thirty, in my office."

I suggested that Willy, who knew the fräulein, would be a better messenger.

"No DP carries messages for my platoon. Why's he hanging out here, anyway? It's time he went home."

"I'm not sure he has a home."

"He's Dutch, isn't he?"

"I don't know if any of his people are left."

"Let him go wherever he wants to go, but I want him out of here. He can make trouble someplace else."

I asked what trouble Willy was making. Everyone was involved in the black market. Everyone traded PX rations.

"Come on, Leo. I'm not blind. I know what's going on. I'm not talking K rations and cigarettes."

An inquiry had reached Battalion and been brought to his attention by Captain Dillon concerning illegal stamp purchases. Names from our platoon had come up. The captain had so far blocked the investigation, pointing to the First Platoon's outstanding combat record. No one was eager to push the inquiry, but if the captain found that a DP was behind the money laundering, he'd throw the book at all those named.

< 168 >

"For his sake and yours, tell Willy to clear out of Grossdorf."

"Why for my sake?"

"Come on, Leo. I know he's your pal."

I delivered the lieutenant's message to Fräulein Hartmann. When my German became tangled she said, in a haughty British accent, "You may speak English."

It must have required a lifetime nurtured by a sense of royal prerogative to cultivate her deep contralto voice of command. I felt awe and resentment.

I told her that we wished to make amends for the damage to her garden. My officer invited her to come see him in the evening at eighteen-thirty, if she was available.

She asked the name of the officer.

"Lieutenant Klamm."

A lieutenant? She shrugged. It was not possible for her to enter her ancestral home while it was occupied. A meeting was no doubt necessary, not only to deal with the matter of her garden, but more important to discuss the status of the factory. She invited the lieutenant to her temporary residence outside Grossdorf. "If he is prepared to see me this evening, that is fine for me also." He could pick her up at the factory. "Inform the lieutenant I have no need for a translator."

I TOLD LIEUTENANT KLAMM the fräulein expected him at her place. He could pick her up at the plant.

"The hell you say." After a pause he asked, "What's your impression?"

"She says you don't have to bring a translator. Just the two of you. She speaks excellent English."

< 169 >

"What do you make of her?"

"Formidable. Top brass."

"Not bad-looking, would you say?"

"Pretty good-looking for a factory owner."

"We got to do something about that damn garden."

After retreat, the lieutenant, wearing pressed ODs, boots polished, a bottle of wine in hand, drove the jeep to the factory side of the fence. Fräulein Hartmann was waiting and climbed in. They took off and Roy Jones yelled, "See the medic when you get back!"

THE GARDEN REPAIRS began within a few days. Maintenance workers cleared the ground, brought in sets of baby lettuce, tomato plants, boxes of annuals— petunias, violets, pansies, marigolds. I don't know where the vegetables and flowers came from—it must have been high priority to bring them in—but the fräulein was back watering. She kept it up for a couple of days and then an ancient maintenance worker in uniform pants, stained shirt, and crumpled army cap took over.

Lieutenant Klamm left each evening on what he called village business. Willy said he was with Gretchen Hartmann, outside Grossdorf.

I asked Willy how many cigarettes the lieutenant would need for the fräulein.

"She is beyond cigarettes. She is more than what a simple lieutenant, looking for a ceremonial blade, can manage."

"Maybe he'll get lucky and stir her heart."

"The heart is one organ of Gretchen Hartmann's that has not been known to stir."

< 170 >

I thought of how Sergeant Lucca had been able to keep the lieutenant in check, guiding him in his obligations, controlling his impetuousness. It was Lucca's platoon until his death, the lieutenant usually deferring to him. The lieutenant needed someone like Lucca, conservative and careful, to rein him in. Lucca would have warned him he was in over his head with Fräulein Hartmann. She was precisely located, the least displaced person in all of Saxony. She had no doubt about the future or her role in it.

"She will devour him in two bites," Willy predicted. He knew her priorities and her intense focus. She meant to keep the factory intact, the machinery maintained, the core of her labor force in place. She needed shelter and food for more than a hundred workers. She needed petrol and oil. She needed information about the future of Chemnitz, of which Grossdorf was a mere satellite. If Chemnitz was to be Russian she would have to find other markets and sources of supply and that's how she would use the lieutenant. She had already approached Willy for help.

"What did you tell her?"

"I said, *'Meisterin,* in the past you have owned my labor. Now I work for myself.'"

We met her one afternoon at the town square, outside the camera shop. My camera used an odd-sized film we were trying to locate.

We entered the camera shop as she was leaving.

"Quite an actor, aren't you?" she said to Willy.

"I stay alive."

"You didn't trust me? A Jew in our midst. I suppose it is

< 171 >

better you kept it to yourself. I knew you were strange."
She smiled, patted his cheek. "Come see me, pretty Willy."

He shrugged. After she left he said that she had probably learned his ID from Lieutenant Klamm.

"Why would he tell her?"

"He hopes to amuse her."

WE SAW HER maintenance crew busy in the garage, working on vehicles she had somehow induced the Wehrmacht to leave behind. Parts came from a motor pool in the forest, full of abandoned Wehrmacht vehicles. Access to the motor pool required military approval and her requests were granted. She was preparing for the day when the rail would be open, the factory adapted to a new market, shipments renewed.

The lieutenant was seen driving her into the forest. She sat beneath a thirty-caliber water-cooled machine gun that was poised behind her on an anchored pedestal.

Roy Jones was at the checkpoint when the lieutenant stopped and introduced the guard detail to Fräulein Hartmann, whom he identified—as if they didn't know—as the executive of the textile factory, no doubt hoping they'd consider the drive official business. She greeted Roy coolly, no concession that they had ever met. Roy spotted a closed picnic hamper in back.

"Going flower picking?"

The lieutenant reddened, said they were headed to the German motor pool, and stepped on the gas.

Roy called after her, "Don't soil that nice blouse, ma'am."

< 172 >

"Thank you," she called back. "Have no fear."

She opened the lieutenant's eyes to a larger world than any he could have known from the vantage point of Massillon, Ohio. He viewed the panorama of the East-West conflict as seen by Gretchen Hartmann. When the Russians were reported to be a few days from our lines, we speculated about what would happen when they arrived. The lieutenant said, "The alliance won't last. World War Three begins."

I asked, "With us and the Germans on the same side?"

He had never seemed a political man. "Bolshevik" and "Wehrmacht" weren't words we expected him to use. Her voice issued from his mouth. He argued with the firm belief of a convert that there would be a confrontation between the civilized West and the barbaric East. He predicted that one day, the factory next door would be producing both GI and Wehrmacht gear.

I told Willy that our naive lieutenant had become the tool of Gretchen Hartmann.

"It's Gretchen Hartmann you should feel sorry for."

"Why?"

"The Russians will be even more terrible to gardens than Roy Jones."

I came across her on the forest road, above the town. She was sitting in the cab of a stalled German truck, a power loom lashed upright to the bed of its chassis. The hood was up, the elderly driver bent into the engine. She waved me over and stepped out of the truck. "Leo?" I didn't expect her to have remembered my name. She was wearing slacks and a sweater. "We have a little trouble here. Perhaps you can help."

< 173 >

I told her I didn't know anything about engines.

"We need—what do you call it? Something for the distributor. *Ja?*" she called to her driver, who was bent under the hood. He came up holding a dull metal cap in his hands, pointed to wires. I'm sure she could have given me lessons about every part of an engine. Her English limped when she wanted to show herself vulnerable. "Maybe you can ask Lieutenant Klamm if he can send us some help?"

I brought the message to the lieutenant and he drove to her rescue. The next day she waved to me from the factory side of the fence, "*Danke,* Leo."

I shouted back, *"Bitte, Fräulein,"* to the clear disgust of Roy Jones.

< 174 >

CHAPTER 10

< RUSSIANS >

To the east beyond Grossdorf there was a large plain, once cultivated, but fallow for more than a year, old furrows eroded, almost leveled. You could see for a mile across this plain, as far as the tall stacks of Chemnitz.

Chemnitz was abandoned, waiting to be taken. It was the third largest city in Saxony, known since medieval times for its textiles. Chemnitz pioneered machine construction, producing machine tools, railroad locomotives, textile machinery. It was a plum and we could have walked into its center at any time without resistance, but Chemnitz was meant for the Russians, and our only view of it was at a distance.

A vanguard of refugees crossed the empty plain with news of the Russian advance. At first we stopped them at the checkpoint, asked a few questions to make sure they weren't soldiers in civilian garb, then let them pass through, but as the flood increased we were told to hold them at the border.

Among those early refugees was an elderly man bearing

a massive pack, wrapped in oilcloth, bound in a network of rope. He stooped under the burden and didn't straighten when he halted at our checkpoint. He looked at me with beggar eyes and I told him to rest and put down his pack.

I asked whether he had seen Russian soldiers.

"Heh?" He looked at his wife, a shawled, heavyset woman dressed in black, her ruddy, weathered face framed by the black shawl. She got the drift of my question and repeated it to him.

Gray with fatigue, cheeks red at the bone, he eased the pack down and sat on it. He used a pidgin German to make himself understood. *"Zu alt,"* he said. Too old. *"Kein schlafen."* No sleep. His wife dropped her quilt-swaddled bundle, pulled a bottle of water from one of the folds, offered the old man a drink, and after he swigged, took her turn, raw lips fixed to a wine bottle filled with water, her throat pumping—a sturdy woman with thick, chapped hands.

She answered for her husband. *"Sie kommen,"* her voice hoarse with fatigue. They're coming.

"Wer kommt?"

"Die Russen kommen. Schrecklich," she said. The Russians are coming. Terrible.

I asked the man if he'd been a soldier.

"Nein, nein. Zu alt." A farmer, he said. He had another drink and then talked and I got used to his German, which he studded with, *"Verstehen sie?"* Do you understand?

He farmed land a few kilometers from Chemnitz. He had three sons, all prisoners on the Western Front. *"Danke Gott,"* he said.

< 176 >

Better than if they were on the Eastern Front?

"Sie sind barbarisch, die Russen." The Russians are barbarians.

"Schrecklich," the old lady said.

He said the Russians arrived at their farm in the late afternoon. The old couple heard the sound of their approach, grabbed the packs they had earlier prepared, and hid in the woods. They stayed hidden through the night. The Russians came endlessly in ragtag units, gathering in the fields, trampling the early grass, tanks and horse wagons destroying the fields. The farmer described them as a drunken mob, singing and howling. The German lines were in front of the town, in the valley below. The farmer said he'd seen the Wehrmacht troops dig in, kids and old men led by a few regular army. In the morning the Russians prepared for the assault. They were marshaled into one line that spread through all the fields on the heights— through acres of new wheat and alfalfa, through the neighbors' fields—on and on and on, horse and wagon and tank and truck and artillery and cavalry and foot soldiers. The artillery set off a ferocious barrage. The sound of hell, the old man said. *Shrecklich!* said the old lady. Then came a vast surge, a wave of Russian soldiers in tan and dark brown tunics—drunk, singing, howling—advancing behind smoke and fire. The noise filled every corner of the world, only gradually receding as the line plunged down the slope. There seemed little discipline in the attack. You couldn't tell who led or who followed; there was no apparent concern for losses. It was, as the old couple described it, an ecstasy of slaughter and ruin.

< 177 >

The boys and old men below had no chance. Those who survived the shelling ran from their trenches, abandoning weapons and gear, heading into town. The Russians caught them, swarmed over them. The surge kept on through the town and beyond toward Chemnitz. It wasn't until deep night, when there was no longer any sound of battle, that the old couple stumbled down the hill, following a path of ruin. Fields were destroyed, the town still burning. The dead were heaped everywhere, soldiers and civilians. The survivors said women had been raped on the spot.

So the old folks told me. I sent them to the train station, where they would be able to put down their packs and scrounge for food and drink. They were among the fortunate. The refugees who came later weren't allowed to pass through our lines.

With stories like these, just the rumor of a Russian approach was enough to empty towns. The townsfolk brought whatever they could load into knapsacks and carts and made for our lines. They pulled carts by hand for lack of horses. They pushed vehicles out of gas. They crossed the field between Chemnitz and Grossdorf, warning that the enemy was coming fast behind them.

They begged for sanctuary. We wouldn't let them through. Our orders were to halt German civilians until Military Government arrived to weed out any war criminals who might be among them masquerading as refugees, or soldiers passing as civilians. Keep them all at the border, we were told.

The refugees pleaded with us to let them into Grossdorf. They were stopped by rolls of barbed wire on the

< 178 >

perimeter of our checkpoint. Our guards had a clear field of vision left and right and were prepared to shoot.

We told the refugees to wait for Military Government. "When do they come?"

"No idea."

"We cannot stay in this field. We need food and water."

There was no sanitation. They risked typhus and cholera and, worse than cholera, the Russians.

I took my turn at the main roadblock as an interpreter. I said what I was told to say. Halt. No entry. We don't know who you are. You could be soldiers disguised as civilians. You could be spies. You could be war criminals. You have to wait here for Military Government to sort you out.

The replies were almost always the same. We are poor villagers, ordinary citizens, not Nazis. We have lost everything. *Alles kaput.* A plague on Hitler.

They said it now, only after defeat, the Russians on their tails. I steeled myself to be hard-hearted but sometimes it was too much.

A man in striped pajamas, concentration-camp garb, reached our checkpoint. He spoke directly to me with begging eyes, "I am trying to go home."

He was tall and dark. He could have been Jewish or Hungarian or Romanian or, for that matter, German. He was not in bad shape, other than obvious fatigue. He didn't have a prison-camp pallor. He had intelligent, gentle eyes and looked closely at me as if he spied kin. I turned away, deferred to Novak, head of the guard detail, a ponderous, careful man. I relayed the refugee's appeal and pointed to his garb.

< 179 >

Novak shook his head. "How do we know he is what he says?"

"By the clothes he's wearing. I think he's okay."

"The clothes are clean and he's in pretty good shape. Tell him he has to wait for Military Government."

I told him he had to wait until someone with authority could check his identity.

"I only wish to go home. You can see what I am."

He claimed to be Hungarian. I said there were Hungarian fascists.

"Do I look like a fascist?"

"I do not have the authority to let you through. I'm sorry."

I offered him a can of C-ration ham and eggs.

He smiled, "Thank you," and disappeared into the crowd. My instinct had been to let him pass. The soft voice, the sorrowful smile seemed identity enough. I could have let him slip through. Other guards, bribed with sex and loot, had allowed refugees into Grossdorf. I saw him squatting near the water, digging into the C rations. When Novak left for a break I motioned him over. I turned my back and spoke softly.

"I am inspecting my medicine bag. If you pass behind me I will not see you. Move fast—*schnell*—into the trees. When I turn around you will be gone."

He said, "God thank you," and I didn't think that was a Jewish response and realized I could be making a mistake.

Novak returned. "Did you let that guy through, Leo?"

"What guy?"

"He's probably okay. But don't pull that again, pal."

< 180 >

I told the captain I didn't want to serve at the border. I was a medic, a noncombatant, obliged to tend all wounded, friend or foe, without distinction. I wasn't here to tell refugees they were barred from safe haven.

Captain Dillon said it was a lousy job for everyone and interpreters were in short supply and to stick with it.

Military Government never showed up. Their resources were stretched thin and there were more important places than Grossdorf. The once-empty field between Grossdorf and Chemnitz was crammed with desperate people. Tarps and rain gear were stretched from wagons. A makeshift city came into being with a population perhaps larger than Grossdorf's. The citizens of this new town huddled under canvas during rains, fueled their campfires with anything that burned. They had the use of a well near the post. They only had the provisions they had brought with them.

WE HEARD A different view of the Russian advance from liberated Allied PWs. A band of ragged French soldiers marched into Grossdorf under an improvised tricolor, singing the "Marseillaise." Contingents of British, imprisoned since Dunkirk and Arnhem, also came through our checkpoint followed by GIs, penned up since the German breakthrough at the Bulge. The Red Cross was on hand to usher the Allied PWs home.

I told an Englishman who reached our lines what the German farmer had said about Russians in battle. That wasn't his experience. His camp was liberated by Russian troops, and the freed prisoners were carried along into battle, so he'd seen the Soviets in action.

< 181 >

He was a tall, very thin officer, bristle-bearded, wearing a soiled garrison cap and ragged uniform, wobbling with fatigue. He was scheduled for immediate transport to a railhead and would be in a field hospital within hours.

He had been with the Russians during just such an assault as the German farmer had described. He said the old man's account was accurate to a point. The Russians swarmed down on the enemy with seeming indifference to casualties. The demoralized German troops broke and fled. And, yes, there was no sparing the Germans. He could believe the stories of rape and ruin. The Russians could be brutal, fueled with vodka. But he had little sympathy for the victims. Life in PW camps had been grim. The prisoners were held under deadly discipline and starvation rations. On the way to our lines they had met DPs released from extermination camps and had heard the first reports of genocide. You couldn't pity the Germans when you heard what they had done. As for the Russians, they were impulsive, often drunk, and it was tough being their enemy, but they were generous, exuberant friends.

"Barbarians?"

"Maybe you could say that. But if they are, better barbarians than civilized, murderous krauts."

Lieutenant Klamm summoned us to hear the amended nonfraternization orders. We were not to have dealings with Russian soldiers when they reached us save for official business. We weren't to go behind their lines; they weren't to pass through ours. The intention was to keep the two sides apart. The brass was concerned that an incident —a drunken quarrel, a confusion of cultures—might

< 182 >

touch off a larger conflict. Yanks and Russkies weren't natural allies.

We stayed in Grossdorf, listening for the sound of the Russians, expecting to hear the stormy approach of a long line of barbarians.

The actual coming caught us unawares.

ONE AFTERNOON A single wagon came up our driveway, pulled by a plodding horse. Aboard were three Russian soldiers. The driver was a hefty woman, red-cheeked and beaming, bobbed brown hair beneath a dark beret. She wore a brown military tunic and skirt and ankle-high stomper boots. Seated beside her was a trim aristocratic-looking soldier in a light tan tunic with epaulettes, wearing an overseas cap; his knees were crossed and black leather glistened along his calves. He was slim, blond, elegant. He smoked a cigarette gripped in a holder, his demeanor more suited to a command car than a ramshackle hay cart.

The third soldier, also blond, wore a tan tunic and dark brown pants. He was tall and rigid. He held an automatic weapon—the sort we called grease guns—at the ready. After hugs and handshakes he relaxed, put down his weapon, took out his camera.

It was not an official contact. The three Russians had been wandering over new terrain and had entered Grossdorf without authorization, bypassing our guard. The official encounter had occurred elsewhere, at the Elbe River, with high brass present, the meeting filmed and viewed worldwide. Grossdorf wasn't even a sideshow.

I assumed the elegant Russian was an officer because

< 183 >

of his epaulettes and manner of command. The cigarette holder contributed to the effect. He was delighted to receive American cigarettes and in return offered an open bottle of vodka. We passed around his bottle, brought out beer and glasses. The Russian raised his glass. *"Zum Sieg,"* he said. To victory. We clinked glasses and bottles. His underling produced his camera and we brought out ours. We snapped the Russians; they snapped us. I was photographed holding the Russian automatic weapon. I passed the gun to Novak, who had his photo taken. The Russians were snapped holding our M1s.

"The great war has ended," the Russian officer said. "The Wehrmacht has vanished between us. We meet as brothers." He shook my hand, insisted on a photo of the handshake.

Lieutenant Klamm remained apart from the celebration, gave no hugs, shook no hands. He motioned me over.

"Find out what they're doing in Grossdorf."

I asked the Russian officer if there was anything he wanted.

He said, "We are only looking." He asked what sort of building the factory was and I told him.

"There are other factories here?"

Grossdorf was a city of farmers, and this was the only factory.

"That is your officer?" He nodded toward Lieutenant Klamm on the porch. I said, "Yes." Before taking off, the Russian went around the platoon shaking hands and ignored Klamm. I offered the buxom woman soldier a comradely embrace and she squeezed back vigorously. The

< 184 >

Russians climbed aboard their wagon, the officer lit up for the road and waved his cigarette holder. *"Auf Wiedersehen."* The horse reared, the woman giggled, leaned forward, walloped the horse on its rump, and our first Russians were gone. The end of the war had snuck up on us by horse and wagon.

The lieutenant asked what the Russian wanted with our factory.

"He wanted to know what kind of building it was."

"It's none of his damn business. He isn't supposed to be here. I don't know how he got past our guards."

Novak said they hadn't come through our posts. They must have gone around the city and come in from the west.

We heard from Captain Dillon that these chance meetings were happening up and down the line. The Russians were already in Chemnitz and these encounters were likely to go on for a long time. We were to stay calm and avoid incidents. "They have a problem with discipline. Shake hands and get them back to their lines without starting World War Three."

A few days later there was a second encounter. Again the guard was bypassed. This time it was a single, unarmed Russian soldier on foot. He came down the street wearing a tan tunic and puffy pants and high boots, a little fellow without a hat, his straw-colored hair shooting straight out and looping straight down. He was hauling a very large German farmer by the ear. The farmer had to stoop to accommodate the grip.

It was an odd scene, the middle-aged farmer twice the

< 185 >

size of the Russian, who looked to be no more than seventeen or eighteen years old. They stumbled together down the street, the farmer not resisting. They stopped two or three times; the soldier braced to get footing, swung with his free hand, landed solid blows we could hear thirty yards away. The farmer reeled back but made no effort to escape. We came out to intercede.

The soldier beamed at the sight of us. "Comrades!" he said, *"Americanski. Chères amis."* He was a handsome, freckled young man, his remarkable straw hair as straight as broom bristles.

I asked, *"Was ist los?"*

He said, in German, "Please. I have no gun. Let me borrow a gun."

I asked why he wanted a gun.

"To kill this man."

He twisted the German's ear. The farmer grimaced but made no sound.

"Why do you want to kill him?"

"He called me a barbarian."

"You want to kill him for that?"

He told us he was away at school when the Germans came to his village. They raped his mother and sisters and cut their throats. He learned how his family died from surviving neighbors. Now this man called him a barbarian and he intended to kill him and go back to his house and rape his wife.

"He will be punished," I said. "Leave him with us."

"You will punish him?"

"Certainly."

< 186 >

He let go the farmer's ear. He loved *Amerikanskis,* he said, and embraced me and pounded my back. "We are comrades?"

I assured him we were and that I would see to it the farmer was punished. He hugged me again. He hugged Roy Jones and Novak. Then he waved farewell and headed toward the farmhouse.

"He is crazy," the farmer said. "He wants to kill me."

I asked if he had indeed called the soldier a barbarian.

"He does not understand German. He is crazy."

The shaken farmer stayed with us the rest of the afternoon.

I told Roy Jones and Novak what had happened.

Roy said, "Why didn't you let him kill the son of a bitch? I'd have lent him my gun."

Novak nodded.

"What is it with you, Doc?" Roy asked. "You'd think you, of all people, would want to see these bastards dead."

I guessed he meant, You, Doc, a Jew, are too softhearted to operate in this world. You need coldhearted sons of bitches like me to keep things straight in this world. I sometimes thought Roy was right and that I let others do what I didn't have the heart to do. But all in all I followed my heart and was glad I was a medic without a gun to use or lend.

THE THIRD RUSSIAN encounter was with a little sergeant, lean and weathered and tough-looking. He wore a cap with a bill, almost too large for his sharp, creased face. Even though the weather was mild, he was dressed in a

< 187 >

dark, heavy wool coat that almost reached the ground. I guessed his rank from the knobs on the shoulders of his greatcoat and the holstered sidearm hanging from one side of a pistol belt. There was a black leather scabbard with a blade on the other side of the belt.

He came to us driving a German vehicle with a puny rear engine that putt-putted in idle. He had come to our quarters looking for gas.

I checked with the lieutenant.

"Give him a can of gas and get rid of him. "

The Russian understood from the tone that the lieutenant was no friend.

Emptying the five-gallon GI can into his tank, he asked, "You like him, your officer?"

"He is a good man, but sometimes hard."

"He is not a good man. They are none of them good, not Russian officers, not American officers. Only the common soldiers are good."

I told him he spoke the truth.

"Common people everywhere are good," he said.

"Germans, too?"

Germans were animals, not men. Murderers. His unit had liberated camps. "The Germans are no good. Not true?"

"Yes, true." To get rid of him I agreed with everything he said.

"The common Russian soldier, the common American soldier are brothers, not true?"

"Yes, true."

"I will show you a place, here in this village where Russki and *Amerikanski* can drink together."

< 188 >

"I need my officer's permission."

I told Klamm the man wanted to take me somewhere for a drink.

"Just get rid of him. Go with him if you have to but don't let him take you out of town."

The little German car was low-powered and noisy. We drove to a hotel that might have been appropriate to the Midwest, the only one in town, just off the square, a non-descript two-story wood building, paint faded and blis-tered. Willy had told me it was a place where farmers stayed when they came to Grossdorf to do business at the bank or market. It had apparently been taken over by DPs. Inside the dingy lobby I recognized several Russians whom I had seen hanging around the town square. The lobby was stripped, not even a chair, no wall hangings or carpets. The DPs stood in the middle of the room. A few squatted against the wall. The place was dense with to-bacco smoke. They rolled their own. To smoke ready-mades would have been to burn money.

We climbed a bare stairway, threads of carpet snagged in nails, and entered a room on the second floor, empty save for a small, battered oak table and two unsteady chairs. The walls were grimy with patches of white where pictures had been removed. The wide plank floor was scuffed and splintered, the windows almost opaque with caked dirt.

The sergeant motioned me to sit and took the chair across from me. He didn't bother to remove his coat or cap or pistol belt. A woman came in, bearing two mugs and two plates on a tray. She wore a Russian tunic, her hair

< 189 >

bound in a shawl. It was Katrina, whom I hadn't seen since we first arrived in Grossdorf.

"Katrina?"

She didn't answer and I thought it was possible I'd made a mistake. That Katrina was vital and angry, expecting redemption when her *Kavalieren* arrived. This woman was subdued and sullen.

"Katrina?"

She looked at me, gave no sign of recognition, but it was definitely her, handsome and voluptuous.

"Your cavaliers have come," I said. "Do you have justice?"

She shrugged and left the room. It was clearly Katrina, and when the Russian sergeant asked how I knew her, I understood from his tone that it did her no favor to be associated with me. It might have been dangerous for her to acknowledge we knew each other.

I said she resembled a woman I had met. I was probably mistaken. I told him about the *lager* and how I had helped get provisions for the Russian women.

He was only interested in food and drink for us. "We have nothing to eat. Let us drink, then we will go out."

He pulled a bottle from an inner pocket of his coat. It was the shape and size of a bottle of rubbing alcohol, containing a clear liquid, the penciled word *"spiritus"* taped to it. He half-filled my mug, then his. He reached into another pocket of his greatcoat and brought out a small bread and a skinny sausage. *"Kielbase,"* he said. He pulled the blade from his scabbard, a beautiful ceremonial weapon. He sliced the bread, sliced the sausage, placed portions on

< 190 >

my plate, then on his. He wiped the blade on his coat sleeve, then laid it on the table. He took a bite of bread and sausage, then a deep swig from his mug and bade me do the same. The sausage was hard and spicy and needed intense chewing. The drink was savage, with a gasoline odor, and I was almost immediately nauseated. He finished his drink and I felt obliged to do the same. He wanted to pour again. I pulled away my mug but he insisted we commemorate the victory of the brotherhood of common soldiers. I reluctantly offered my cup and he poured the *spiritus*.

His judgments were immediate and strong, not easy to oppose. He didn't seem affected by the drink, while I had to concentrate to keep my focus. Our limited German made no great demands but I was barely able to manage my end of the dialogue.

I complimented him on the blade. "A beautiful weapon."

"You like?"

He held it up for me. An inscription was etched on the face of the blade that I was too blurred to make out. Above the inscription a marvelous spread-winged eagle was engraved.

"Silver and steel," the sergeant said. "No good for war. Good for *kielbase*."

He admired my watch, an inexpensive Mickey Mouse watch I'd bought through the PX. He said such a watch was very desirable in the Soviet Union.

I stripped it off and gave it to him.

He bent across the table, kissed my forehead, removed

< 191 >

his pistol belt and pulled away the scabbard. He extended blade and scabbard to me. "For you, my friend."

I said, no, no, no. It was too valuable.

"We are brothers."

He fitted the scabbard to my belt, strapped the watch to his wrist, the barter consummated. He finished his drink, motioned me to do the same. After the gift, I couldn't refuse.

"Come. We eat."

I stumbled against him, clutched the rickety railing going downstairs. He held my arm, led me through the lobby.

I remember being driven to the Bahnhof restaurant. The chilly station was jammed with refugees camping amid knapsacks and suitcases—women and children, a few old men, the smell stale and sour. They wore ski pants, wool jackets, beaked caps, stocking hats. The station restaurant was empty. An elderly waiter in white shirt and black suit came from the kitchen to tell us that sometimes they were open, more often closed, and today there was no food. The Russian pulled out his pistol, pounded the butt on the table. *"Essen!"* he shouted.

The waiter said, *"Gar nichts zu essen, mein Herr. Alles kaput."* There's nothing to eat.

The sergeant raised his pistol and fired into the ceiling. Plaster showered down, doused the black-suited waiter. The shot silenced the railroad station.

"Please. I beg you," the waiter said. "I will find you something to eat."

We were served but I have no idea what we ate. Everything tasted gassy and explosive. I barely recall the drive

< 192 >

back to the Schloss. I threw up in the driveway and fell
down. The little man hoisted me up and supported me past
my outraged lieutenant and amused buddies, who pointed
to my bedroom. He dumped me in bed, kissed my forehead, said, *"Auf Wiedersehen,"* got into his gassed-up car,
and putt-putted toward the Russian lines.

I HAD ACQUIRED the wherewithal that would allow
Willy to remain in Grossdorf. The lieutenant had ordered
Willy to clear out. He'd gone into hiding, and I found him
at Ingrid Schultz's and brought him the ceremonial blade.

"Is this what Klamm was looking for?"

He inspected the blade, asked where I got it, then offered me thirty dollars.

I told him it was a gift, but he refused to accept a gift.
He insisted on a transaction. He asked what I'd paid.

"My Mickey Mouse watch," I told him.

"You made yourself a good deal." He removed his own
watch, a solid gold Swiss. His principle of quid pro quo
demanded a barter and I accepted the watch.

Willy showed up at the Schloss that night.

"I have found it for you, Lieutenant."

He presented Klamm with the newly polished, glistening
black scabbard. The lieutenant removed the blade, held it to
the light, turned it horizontally to inspect the engraving.

Willy translated the Gothic inscription. *"'Zur Errinerung
an Meine Dienstzeit.'* To the memory of my service. This is
what you wanted, sir?"

"It's a beauty. What are you asking?"

"For you, a carton of cigarettes."

< 193 >

"A deal." Klamm went to his room with blade and scabbard and returned with a carton of Lucky Strikes, his collection now complete.

Dear Folks, I'm sending along photos of our meeting with Russian soldiers. You'll note that in one photo I'm shaking hands with a Russian officer. He's looking directly at me while I'm grinning at the camera. My friend Novak says the Russians took the same photo and when it appears in Pravda the text will say, look at brave Ivan, greeting the *Amerikanski* ally with full heart, and now look at decadent Amerikanski ally, only interested in propaganda opportunity. This war is almost over. I yearn for home.

< 194 >

CHAPTER 11

< MAY 8 >

We tidied up, war grime erased, faces scraped, hair slicked back, shoes polished, clothes freshly laundered, ready to party. We blocked the street in front of Schloss Hartmann with chairs and tables. Holiday fare came from the company kitchen located in a nearby village. Metal vats held turkey and potatoes and salad, a massive urn for the coffee. We had apple pie and vanilla ice cream for dessert. An assistant cook ladled out the main dish into mess kits. Beer was tapped from a keg, bottles of wine on every table.

Lieutenant Klamm banged a canteen cup on his table to get our attention. He was a big man, flushed from a few beers, his trim mustache and severe crew cut barely maturing his teenage face. When we were silent he announced in the stentorian voice developed for the parade ground that on this eighth day of May 1945, the Germans had officially surrendered. There might be a detour to Tokyo but sooner or later we would be en route home. He reviewed again the stations of our combat journey, northern France, Belgium, Luxembourg, the Sauer, the Siegfried line, the

Rhine, and at the end, Grossdorf. We had weathered it all, suffered losses, and become one family.

He drummed into us that our journey would never be forgotten and that we were joined forever.

We'd heard that refrain before. It meant much to Klamm to believe that somehow we were fused and the platoon would never end.

He told us to fill our canteen cups and toast the U.S. Army and then our company and above all our platoon. We raised our cups, cheered the U.S. Army. Hurray! Our company. Hurray! The First Platoon. Hurray! What began as a kind of mocking deference to Klamm's sentimentality deepened as we clinked cups, and the last cheer was heartfelt. Stunned by beer, wine, the sun, it felt like the Fourth of July and I think we all believed for a moment that we'd never forget, and so, never be parted, and when Klamm read aloud the names of the dead—Sergeant Lucca first and foremost—it wasn't only the loss of our dead that made us tearful, but the tipsy love of each other. We raised our cups, strongly joined.

Then an abrupt change of tone. Klamm had an announcement. A GI musical, *Alles Kaput,* was appearing in Zwickau, Maurice Sully a star of the show. Klamm didn't know when we were scheduled to attend; he imagined soon. Attendance was voluntary, but who would want to miss Maurice on stage? He believed that someday Maurice would be a show business headliner, someone we would be proud to claim as our own.

"The war in Europe is over," he shouted. "Eat, drink, and enjoy!"

< 196 >

We cheered, whooped, shook hands, hugged. An hour later, drunk and sated and happy, we ignored the fact that Japan was undefeated and the war in the Pacific still beckoned. We changed into fatigues and went to the meadow behind the *Schloss* for a game of softball.

Afterward I was sleepy and still high and prickly with sweat and meadow dust, but I didn't want to return to the *Schloss* and lose the holiday mood. I walked with Novak to the village center to pick up some more photos of Russian soldiers.

Grossdorf was tranquil. There were a few DPs waiting at the square, but otherwise nothing moved.

Novak called this a great day, as strong a statement of feeling as I could expect from him. He seemed confident about where he had been and how he would end up. He was the man we asked to mediate our arguments. He'd grin and tell you to figure it out for yourself. His refusal to be involved seemed evidence of wisdom.

Almost from the time we arrived in Grossdorf, Novak had shacked up with Carla, a tiny, blond widow from Chemnitz. Novak spoke a few words of German. Her English was barely decipherable. They walked arm in arm near the *Schloss* in open disregard of the nonfraternization order, and that didn't seem wise. Novak went to her each night, bringing rations, like a family man.

He already had a family in Wisconsin. A wife and child waited on a farm outside Lacrosse for his return. How many wives could a judicious man have? All he would say about Carla when we needled him about his Grossdorf ménage was that she was very clean, as though that unre-

< 197 >

markable quality was justification for setting up house. What he may have meant was, she was dainty and tidy and he'd been in combat with rank men for six months and when relief was offered he couldn't refuse. I asked him on the way to the town center if Carla knew he was married.

"She knows."

"It's okay with her?"

"Well, that's how it is."

I asked what would happen to her when he returned to Wisconsin. He said he'd survived the ordeal of combat and nothing more could worry him.

It was an attitude I wished for, and always the student —trying to find out from anyone how to survive and be happy surviving—I hung around Novak, hoping for lessons in being carefree.

I rattled on about how great I was feeling. I told Novak I didn't know if my love for the platoon would last out the day, but right now I felt the same as Klamm, that we were family. Maybe if in the next hour word reached us that VE Day was a hoax and the war was still on and we were stuck with each other for another six months, I'd feel that the platoon was a prison and that I was only connected to these other inmates by chains. Right now I felt we were brothers. We may have come from different worlds but what we'd been through together made us family.

"Let's see how you feel when you sober up."

"It's not just the wine," I said. How could you not feel intimate if you'd slept together in slit trenches and shit together in straddle trenches?

< 198 >

Novak said, "Thanks, but I'll take my two holer back on the farm."

Straddle trenches were narrow trenches, about a foot wide, two feet deep, a dozen feet long. We squatted face to back, toilet tissue in the webbing of helmet liners, learning each other's stink—"Man, something must have crawled up you and died"—and accepting each other despite the stink and despite the excesses of war.

"I feel terrific," I said. "We're going home. Maybe there are kooks in the family but like that kook Roy says, every family has its kooks."

"You're feeling terrific because you're loaded. There's still the Japs to fight. We got a long way to go."

We were talking outside the camera shop at the town center when we heard a horn honking and saw the jeep barreling toward us. Lieutenant Klamm braked sharply, flung open the passenger door. He barked at me to get in. "Not you," he said to Novak.

Novak asked, "What's wrong?"

"Trouble at one of our posts."

"Is it the Russkis?"

We took off fast, leaving him behind. We headed east, toward Chemnitz.

"A kid's been shot. A seven-year-old boy. He may be dead. I got a call from the guards. I warned the assholes not to fire their weapons. They must have been shooting at deer and a stray hit the kid."

"You think it's our guards?"

"Roy Jones and Alfieri on duty? With screwups like

< 199 >

that, what are the chances it wasn't them? VE Day and this happens! Can you believe it?"

We drove to the edge of Grossdorf. The boy lay on a culvert crossing a few hundred yards from the guard post. A German civilian hovered over him, shielding the body from the child's playmates, three boys and a girl, all about seven or eight. Roy Jones and Alfieri stood nearby, obviously worried. The German civilian seemed to be in his thirties, probably a returned soldier in civvies. He stepped aside, and I knelt by the child, a freckled, sandy-haired boy, mouth open, lips soft, long-lashed eyes closed, and a wound like a large red caste mark in the middle of his forehead, no breath or pulse.

The German calmly said, *"Das Kind ist tot."* The child is dead.

I tipped the boy's face, smoothed aside the light brown hair, looked for an exit wound, but didn't find one.

The lieutenant asked what I thought.

The child wore a broad-striped shirt, green lederhosen, ankle-high boots with rolled white socks—someone's lovely, well-tended child. I handled him as unfeelingly as I did any of the dead. I was cool and unaffected. In retrospect, I'd say, numb and frozen, definitely sobered.

I told the lieutenant I didn't see how a wound so small could have been caused by an M1. There was no exit wound. I'd have expected a thirty-caliber bullet to have blown a hole in the back of the skull. The only scenario I could imagine was that the shot had traveled a great distance and that the bullet was spent. I asked how far away the guard post was.

< 200 >

"Between three and four hundred yards."

"Maybe an M1 could do this from that far away."

Alfieri said, "We aimed into the forest. We didn't shoot this way."

Roy Jones told him to shut up.

Lieutenant Klamm was furious. "You had orders, no shooting! VE Day, a day of celebration, peace in Germany, and you screwups have to bring on big trouble. You see what happens when you disobey orders? You killed a seven-year-old kid!"

Roy and Alfieri looked at each other glumly.

The lieutenant asked where exactly they were when they were shooting. "If you don't want to spend the next few years in the stockade, you'll tell me the truth."

Alfieri said, "We were at the guard post. Ask the Russkis. There were two of them on guard with us. They were shooting, too. Maybe it was a Russki bullet."

"Which way were they shooting? What weapons did they use?"

"They were using grease guns, shooting everywhere."

"Grease guns don't have the range. You're sure they didn't have rifles?"

"Maybe. Ask Roy."

Roy stared coldly ahead. The lieutenant asked, "How about it?"

"They were using grease guns. Nothing else."

"You're sure about that?"

"They didn't use rifles."

"Great. Just great. Now I have to call the CO and who knows where it's going?"

< 201 >

The German civilian, who had been whispering with the children, suddenly cuffed one of the boys, then grabbed him and shook hard. The boy started wailing and that set off the others.

I asked, *"Was gibt?"* Instead of answering, the German shook the boy harder. The child sobbed something I couldn't make out, and the German let go of him, went to the side of the road, sprawled on his belly, stretched below the roadway into the culvert, and came up holding a pistol that fit the palm of his hand. *"Ein Walther,"* he said, naming the tiny weapon he handed to the lieutenant.

The children had found the cute Walther pistol, were playing with it; it went off and the boy was killed. The children who had at first been solemn and quiet now sobbed all out. The civilian gathered them in. He had one of those stern, neutral faces I expect to see on cops. He wore a white shirt, sleeves rolled up, arms tanned and muscular. He stroked their heads, patted them, *"Shhh."*

He'd served with the police before the war. Grossdorf was then a quiet town, he said. Two officers, detached from Chemnitz, were the entire force. There was sometimes trouble with drunken farmers after market day, but nothing that couldn't be easily handled. No need for night duty. The spillover from Chemnitz caused more serious crime, but still nothing of great moment. In his seven years in Grossdorf there had never been a homicide.

I repeated all this to the lieutenant, who was obviously relieved. "This is a civilian matter. Ask him if he's going to take care of it."

The German cop, still sheltering the weeping kids, told

< 202 >

me the child's mother had already been notified. He would wait until she arrived. He agreed to take care of police details.

Klamm asked if the man needed the use of the jeep.

"Thank you. We have transportation."

"Let's get out of here before it gets more complicated." He told Roy and Alfieri he'd sent their relief to the guard post and they could return to the platoon.

I didn't want to ride back with the lieutenant and told him I'd walk to the *Schloss*.

When he was gone, Roy Jones shoved me hard in the chest. "J. Edgar Hoover here says, 'No exit wound. Must be a shot from the guard post.' The son of a bitch is ready to blame his buddies for something they didn't do."

I apologized. Klamm suspected the fatal shot had come from our post and I hadn't thought of other possibilities.

"What the hell do you know about exit wounds?"

I agreed I knew nothing. I told Roy he'd be glad to know I was finished with the aid-man business. "The war's over. If anyone calls for help I'm heading the other way."

"That should save a few lives."

He was satisfied to get in the last word and I wasn't about to quarrel. My days with Roy Jones were numbered.

Before we could take off, the child's mother came running toward us, arms waving, hair flying, shouting something like, "Hansi! Hansi!" I didn't recognize Ingrid Schultz until she was almost at the crossing. She fell to her knees moaning, and clasped the body of her child. The German cop knelt at her side and told her what had hap-

< 203 >

pened. The children had found the weapon, were playing with it, and her son was killed.

She rocked with her child, moaning, *"Mein Kind, mein liebes Kind!"* The other kids were bawling.

I bent down to her and said lamely that I sorrowed for her loss. It must have sounded absurd. She glanced at me with no apparent recognition. I asked the German if there was anything I could do to help. He could think of nothing.

Roy Jones and Alfieri were finished with their duty and eager to return to the platoon and what remained of the celebration.

"They saved us chow," Roy said. "Let's go while it's still saved."

I started back to the *Schloss* with them. Roy was still pissed off that he had been suspected in the killing of the boy. "I know what I was shooting at and I hit what I'm shooting at. I wasn't shooting at no seven-year-old kid."

Alfieri, who was not much of a marksman, agreed. "We were shooting at targets in the woods."

I told them to go on ahead. I wanted to be by myself. "His mother's a friend. I used to bring chocolate for the kid."

"That's something you won't do no more."

I turned into the woods above town, terrifically deflated, as low as I had been high. The platoon brotherhood I had celebrated seemed no more than drunken sentimentality. We accommodated to everything. Being alive was a transient, easily modified condition, no intrinsic joy in it. Killing was simple, dying was scarier than ever. I would return

< 204 >

to Detroit and resume my life. Nothing would have changed except that I'd lost time.

An old resentment boiled up while I stumbled through the woods above town, past the abandoned German motor pool with its scavenged, camouflaged vehicles. What came to mind with sudden vividness was the night they left me in a trench with Lucca and Billy dying and rockets coming in. Everyone ran for cover and I was stuck under rocket fire with the dying men. By the time relief came, fear was rung out of me and I felt as dead as stone. The platoon had abandoned me and no Paris leave could make that right.

I knew it was a stupid grievance. They came for me as soon as the rockets let up. And then wasn't Marishka the true reward? The gods must have placed her near the entrance of the Moulin Rouge and given me the nerve to approach her. In her rue du Bac apartment I unfroze and came alive.

There was no such chance with Ingrid Schultz. We had sex, the kids never around, the blinds always drawn. I asked her not to wear scent and she scrubbed herself plain for our next date, her skin dry, the deep lines in her face apparent, her light hair—the color of her son's hair—pulled back and bound. The next time she dressed in something like ski pants and a white blouse. She offered me a glass of wine. *Danke. Bitte.* I offered her a cigarette. When she bent for an ashtray I brought her to the couch and it was quickly done, no intimacy, nothing said. I was the master, she the occupied, nothing equal in our dealings, and I couldn't get beyond the eroticism of that inequality. Again I came away from her solitary and unrelieved.

< 205 >

Her grief revealed her to me as sex hadn't. I felt ashamed that I'd made so little of her. Novak would have done better.

It no longer felt like victory.

WILLY FRUCHT STOPPED me on a street near the *Schloss*. I hadn't seen him in several days. He waved me over to where he stood out of sight.

He had come to say good-bye. He had decided to leave Grossdorf. He would be in Zwickau for a few days, then, who could tell? Maybe Palestine. Maybe the USA. Never again the Netherlands. He intended one day to go to America and, if so, would look me up in Detroit.

Did he know about Ingrid's child?

He knew.

"Will she be okay?"

He looked at me as if I were a fool. "She will survive. Everyone has lost family. It's a common European experience. You mourn and recover."

"That's all?"

"If you are lucky."

"Where's your family, Willy?"

"All gone," he said.

Willy despised self-confession. It was a habit of mind without survival value and Willy had a passion to survive. He didn't want to talk about Ingrid and my lack of feeling.

"Why should you feel? You are a Jew. She is a German. What do you expect, love and marriage, and you will take her back to Detroit or maybe, even worse, settle in Grossdorf? These people made life hell on earth."

< 206 >

He removed a sleek black Luger tucked inside his shirt. It was in even better condition than the weapon Maurice owned. "I give it to you. It is yours."

I wasn't allowed to carry weapons and anyhow didn't want one.

"Take it. The war is over. It will remind you while you are wallowing in the life of the mind that there is another way to be. This gun is the wisdom I leave you with."

"A gun in my hand instead of an idea in my head?"

"I cannot afford to be caught with this. Take it. It's a gift. Consider it like money in the bank."

"You once told me you never offer gifts."

"I make an exception. But beware. I could one day show up in Detroit and demand payment."

I told him I would love to see him in Detroit. I would treat him as family.

"I don't ask for that."

The last I saw of Willy in Grossdorf he was headed toward the town center. He was by my reckoning nineteen years old, nowhere at home and in constant motion.

I CLIMBED THE factory fence and cut blooms from the garden and brought the flowers and chocolate to Ingrid. I waited outside the house. The neighbors may have disapproved of my being there but they couldn't do anything about it. I saw her coming down the forest road, dressed in black, shawled like a peasant woman, her boots muddy, carrying a bundle of twigs and small branches for kindling. I went to meet her, took the bundle from her, and walked her to her door.

< 207 >

She must have felt that whatever my motive, it was somehow connected to desire. I tried to reassure her that I was only moved by sympathy. At her house she took off her boots. She let me into the house so there wouldn't be a scene.

The chocolate was for her daughter. "Take it. It's for Martha."

She left flowers and chocolate on the little table in the vestibule.

I asked what I could do to help her.

"Nichts."

"Nothing?"

"Gar nichts." Nothing at all.

She was cold and distant. "It is best if you do not come here again."

I thought I had something to offer—sympathy, consolation, chocolate, cigarettes—but she said, "Nothing. Nothing at all."

< 208 >

CHAPTER 12

< LEAVING GROSSDORF >

Grossdorf was our town by dint of conquest and occupation. A few of us, like Novak, had come to have quasi family connections with Grossdorfers. We knew—and the townsfolk certainly knew—that someday there would be a bill presented and Grossdorf would be made to pay for the foreign labor it had abused and the regime it had supported. But we were there to protect them when the day of reckoning came, and with that assurance the town was able to keep operating with Russian units poised at the border.

In late July we were awakened at midnight and summoned to the parlor of the *Schloss*. A first lieutenant from company headquarters was there with orders confining us to quarters, no communication with anyone outside our unit. Saxony had been given to the Russians at the Yalta summit. We were pulling out of town. We had four hours to get out. We had to be gone by morning, our first stop Zwickau, then out of Saxony entirely, and then out of

Europe, a brief stopover in the United States. The invasion of Japan was our final destination. That's what the messenger told us.

He stressed that no one was to leave quarters. Security was paramount. The evacuation was beginning across Saxony. He said, "If the civilians find out we're leaving, we'll face one helluva refugee problem."

We didn't belong here, it wasn't our homeland, but it was a shock to leave so fast, and Lieutenant Klamm exploded. "We're abandoning them to the Reds! It's betrayal!"

The first lieutenant said, "It's decided at the top. We do what we're told, Charley."

As soon as the messenger was out of sight, Klamm bellowed at us to shape up and start packing. He went to the door, looked out, slammed the door. He moved from squad to squad, telling us what could be loaded in barrack bags. He didn't want to see any forbidden loot. We took his advice and didn't show him our loot. He paced the room, flushed, teeth clenched. "Hell," he said, "hell," and went to his room to pack. He came storming out. "No one leaves without my permission, understand!" then rushed back to his room. "Hell!" he said. "Hell!"

"What he really wants," Novak said, "is for someone to sneak out and tell the fräulein."

I asked Novak whether he was going to tell Carla.

"It's against orders, isn't it?"

We were all busy packing; we only had a couple of hours to fit everything into our packs and barrack bags. Most of us were leaving Grossdorf more burdened than

< 210 >

when we first arrived. We didn't intend leaving anything of ourselves at the *Schloss*. We ate whatever was in the kitchen. I didn't see the lieutenant until it was almost time to assemble. He checked us out before the trucks arrived early in the morning, a two-and-a-half-ton for our transport, a three-quarter-ton for our baggage, both trucks domed with camouflage canvas. At four in the morning we received word by radio and assembled out front with our packs and duffel bags.

There was a quarter moon, low in the sky. It was otherwise so dark that at first we didn't see the crowd gathered in front of the *Schloss*. We heard whispers, children whimpering, panicked demands for silence. News of our move was out. The informant could have been someone in the platoon or a citizen of Grossdorf who had heard about withdrawals elsewhere in Saxony. Behind one of our trucks, Carla sat in a jammed wagon that was hitched to an ancient tractor. She sat on what appeared to be a stuffed GI duffel bag. In the space of a few hours, the townsfolk had loaded carts and wagons.

They intended leaving with us. They wanted to be safe in our shadow. They hoped we would shield them from the Russians.

Captain Dillon drove up, honking a path through the villagers. He said the situation was the same at the other company stations. Security had been compromised all up and down the line and we faced a mass exodus.

"Nothing we can do about it. You'll be okay once you get out of town. These folks won't get far with the transport they got."

< 211 >

He told Klamm to make sure the road was clear when the order came to start rolling.

When would that be?

He expected within the next half hour.

We mounted the truck and waited for orders. Hours passed, the day lightened, the crowd of refugees increased. Most of us quickly adjusted to leaving. This was after all only one more town we'd passed through. And grief was coming to Grossdorf. Why stay for it? Katrina and the other women from the *lager* would finally have their justice. The slave laborers who had been tracking their tormentors would now have their revenge. Grossdorf would suffer a small part of the misery Germany had inflicted on the Slavs.

When the word finally came by radio to move out, Klamm, who'd been standing in the jeep searching the crowd, held back as long as he could before giving the order to start up.

Gretchen Hartmann didn't show herself until we were about to roll. She emerged from the crowd wearing her usual outfit—white blouse, black skirt and shoes. Klamm, in the lead jeep, halted the convoy.

"Gretchen!"

She never looked at him. She stood in the driveway of her factory and shouted something in German. It was intense. I could only make out parts of it. "Grossdorf is your home! Do not abandon it! We survived the Americans! We will survive the Russians! Everything is lost if we leave! They will not harm us! They need our work and I will protect you!"

< 212 >

Gretchen Hartmann used slave labor. Gretchen Hartmann served a regime that slaughtered my people. The ar-
rogance of her imperial manner erased anyone beneath
her, and I didn't wish her well. Yet, I could understand
being inspired by this woman. I could understand why
many in the crowd came over to her. If Klamm's commit-
ment to the army hadn't been stronger than his passion
for Gretchen Hartmann he might have joined her band
of Grossdorfers. As it was, he stayed glued to her until
Sergeant George walked over to the jeep.

"We gotta go, Lieutenant, or we'll be stuck in traffic."

Klamm gave the word and we began to move.

I kept my eyes on her as long as she was in sight. The
last I saw of her she had left her flock and entered her garden, watering can in hand, ready to compel the new day to
behave as she wished.

< 213 >

CHAPTER 13

< DISSOLUTION >

Zwickau on the Mulde River was an ancient industrial city with a population, before the war, of more than a hundred thousand. Some of its churches dated from the fourteenth century, and there was a rich history unavailable to us since we were confined to the city center. The residential and industrial sections were off-limits.

The center of Zwickau swarmed with GIs. Our regiment was there as well as units of other divisions. I saw soldiers wearing patches of the Fourth Armored and Eighty-second Airborne and Third Army Headquarters. We were jammed into a small hotel with the rest of the company. A common mess served much of the battalion. There were few German men to be seen, but DPs were everywhere. They served as barbers and maids and kitchen help.

Army business at the company level was suspended and we idled in Zwickau. There were no guard details, no KP, no drill, no morning assembly or calisthenics, no retreat. There was no need for morning sick call at the company level. The Battalion Aid Station was only a block away and a field hospital was set up on the edge of the city. The division post office was nearby and we received our back mail and back pay.

We hoped for an extended leave in the States before crossing to the Asian Theater of Operations and a new, perhaps more ferocious, war. There was no announced policy for getting us home. Our past was finished, our future vague.

At night we went to the USO, a smoky, beery place, the dance floor jammed from early evening until midnight. A German band—a drum, a piano, a saxophone, a trumpet, a very large horn—played bouncy thirties music and slow maudlin tunes. Dancers bumped and jostled through sweaty two-steps. Fräuleins were everywhere, not only on the dance floor, but at the tables and outside in the spill of light.

ONE NIGHT THE music and dancing stopped. An amplified radio voice announced that the president of the United States was about to deliver an important message. Truman came on to tell us in his flat, stumbling, Midwestern accent that a new kind of weapon, an atomic bomb with a force greater than twenty thousand tons of TNT, had exploded over a Japanese city, the city wiped out in a single blow. The Japanese government had been advised to surrender unconditionally or suffer other attacks of this magnitude.

Nagy asked, "How much is twenty thousand tons of TNT?"

< 215 >

I figured it out in terms we could understand. You can carve out a slit trench with a quarter-pound stick of dynamite. You can do four slit trenches with a pound. With 20,000 tons of TNT you could make 160 million slit trenches. With two to a trench, you could put all of the allied armies underground and still have room for the entire U.S. population and then some.

Novak said, "This is it, then."

"What?"

"We're not going to the Pacific."

Three days later a second bomb exploded, and within a week, the Japanese sued for surrender, and we were entirely done with war. Later we learned that the number of dead and injured in Hiroshima and Nagasaki was almost equal to the total number of men in the Third Army.

A SUBDUED KLAMM briefed us after VJ Day. The platoon was to be disbanded, the battalion erased, the division reduced to its skeleton cadre. We were to be reassigned on the basis of a system of points that rewarded us for length of service and combat experience. Those with the lowest point total would remain in Germany. The rest of us would be sent to units going home.

We figured this would happen in weeks, maybe months. But the next day, I was ordered to return to my medical detachment. There was no need for an aid man because there was no need for a platoon; in fact, no need for a medical detachment since the battalion itself was going out of business.

I found as many of my platoon as I could before we

< 216 >

parted, and the parting was a stripping away. I took no addresses and didn't offer mine.

Klamm was stiff and formal, unable to figure out what our future connection should be. "It was an honor serving with you, Corporal." He had no intention of resuming his work as assistant manager at a Kroger's market. "I'm not going back."

He had applied for continued service in the German occupation.

Roy Jones planned to use his severance pay to buy acreage adjoining the family farm. His hair-trigger temper no longer had the same threat; the peacetime Roy sounding no more dangerous than any truculent farmer.

Novak had his Wisconsin farm.

Nagy was promised his old job at Hudson's department store in Detroit, driving a delivery truck. He meant to keep in touch with Maurice Sully. Maurice was still touring with the GI musical, *Alles Kaput,* somewhere near Paris.

Some didn't have a clear agenda and considered idling at government expense.

"And how about you, Leo?"

It was enough to have survived the war. That's what I thought then.

We had slept together, eaten together, killed together, died and survived together. We were joined together as we'd never been with any others, and yet when the platoon that defined us and held us in place—the source of our pride and loyalty—was discarded, we were unglued. It happened overnight in Zwickau.

• • •

< 217 >

I WAS TRANSFERRED to the headquarters unit of another medical detachment and made a clerk. In my few weeks as a clerk I learned the GI way of writing reports. There was a common set of abbreviations—for instance, *w* for "with," *w/o* for "without," *fr* for "from," and so on. Letters were folded three times with the letterhead exposed. I hunted and pecked for a month until the headquarters unit dissolved. A second lieutenant reported for duty just before I was again transferred. He was newly arrived, newly commissioned, saluted the CO sharply. His voice was familiar, and when he turned from the CO, overseas cap in hand, we stared at each other. It was Joe Witty, my nemesis from basic training, a fine-looking second lieutenant, tall and fair and clean-cut. He was delighted to see someone from Michigan, a buddy from basic training. Our conflict hardly dented his memory. He remembered me as the really bright guy who had made a name for himself by handling an amputation on the rifle range.

He had graduated from OCS a few months before. A ninety-day wonder, he admitted, laughing. He was new to Europe, confessed to being homesick. He'd left our original outfit for advanced medical training and then OCS.

We were both in luck, he said.

The division we had both once belonged to was stationed in the Ardennes just before the Battle of the Bulge and was overrun in the initial assault. The division was captured almost intact, including our old medical detachment. Witty had kept in touch with some of the men and heard of the horrors of the PW camp after their release.

< 218 >

I asked about Sergeant Johnson, whose anti-Semitic venom still pained me.

Witty told me everyone despised Johnson. One of the old outfit who'd been captured after the others still had cigarettes when he rejoined the unit in the PW camp. He passed out cigarettes generously, but when Johnson, the craven bully, came begging, he said, "Johnson, I wouldn't give you the sweat off my balls."

I saw Witty several times in the next few days. We never spoke of our fight or the shower room incident. He told me about his training as a surgical technician. After OCS he administered the surgical unit of a post hospital in New Jersey. He was now slated for occupation duty. Afterward he would return to the University of Michigan, attend medical school, join his father's practice.

He envied my combat experience. Mine was the war he had imagined for himself. He'd never been at the front, never even heard artillery fire.

We agreed to meet back in Ann Arbor. It seemed like a good idea then, but we were on different paths, our common history concluded.

I was transferred to a postal unit and made the supply sergeant. It was fall, the nights were cold. The post office was located across from a railroad station. Each night several of us would cross to the railroad station and I'd call out, *"Warm Zimmer,"* warm room, and we'd return with fräuleins in need of warmth. I set up cots in the supply room so we could all be warmed together. That's as much of my supply duties as I remember.

In late fall I applied for a Paris leave.

< 219 >

MARISHKA WAS PART memory and part dream, and when I considered the facts, it didn't make sense to summon up the flesh-and-blood version. More than seven months had passed since our two nights together. She was a sixteen- or seventeen-year-old French girl available to a person of her choosing for twenty dollars a night. Even if I wanted to bring her home to Mom there was no reason for her to come. It wasn't wise to go looking for her with the expectations I had, but I was hardly wise.

I found a room on the fifth floor of a shabby hotel near the rue du Bac. There was a WC midcorridor of each floor, a bath available by payment to the concierge. The trees were bare, the days sunny; chill winds blew off the river. I wore my winter ODs and Eisenhower jacket and wool overseas cap.

I asked the concierge at the Hotel de l'Avenir if she knew a girl named Marishka. The elderly woman couldn't make out what I wanted until I offered her a few francs, and then she didn't recognize the name. She knew few of the women who passed through the hotel. I described Marishka as best I could—very young, very pretty, a student at the Sorbonne.

She roared with laughter. *"Un étudiant ici? Rien à étudier ici que des verges, des tetons, des cons, et des culs."* Nothing to study here but cocks and tits and cunts and asses.

I didn't find her at the Moulin Rouge. I couldn't find her apartment on the rue du Bac. I patrolled the street, hoping either she or Bernard or Annie would show up. The boulangerie was closed. The baker had gone south.

< 220 >

A clerk at a bookstore near the Seine said she was familiar with an Annie and Bernard who lived in the neighborhood. They wrote for a Communist journal and hung out at the Deux Magots.

I sat outside the Deux Magots on the boulevard St. Germain, drinking coffee and brandy, writing letters home.

I did this for three days. I came in the afternoon and sat till dark, positioning myself near the café façade, where I was sheltered from the wind and could see who was entering.

It turned out that Bernard and Annie had passed by several times. It was his voice I finally recognized. They were leaving the café. He spoke in English, the tone bitter and derisive. "A fine mess," he said.

"It was not intentional," she said soothingly. *"Sois sage."* Behave.

"Bernard?"

He wore black cords, a black leather jacket, and a black beret. Annie's brown suede jacket may have been the one Marishka was wearing when we first met at the Moulin Rouge. They were as I remembered them, much alike in appearance—slender, olive-skinned, large Gallic noses, wide mouths.

"You perhaps remember me. I was a friend of Marishka's. Leo, her American."

"Quel Américain?"

"We met in your apartment in early March."

Annie spoke low to him in French and he laughed. "That American."

Annie lightened up at the mention of Marishka. "We

< 221 >

told her to go, she said, *'Non!'* and now she has gone and we miss her. It was grim in the war. She had courage for everything."

I invited them to sit with me for a cognac.

"For a moment," he said. "No cognac."

Annie said, "It should please you to know that among her vast entourage you were someone special."

It greatly pleased me. I asked where she was.

She had left a month before, headed south to what had been the free zone, accompanied by a French soldier in a jeep.

"I thought she might be back in school."

"What school?"

"Wasn't she a student at the Sorbonne?"

They laughed at the idea. Bernard said, "You have to first graduate from kindergarten." Not that she wasn't bright enough to give the impression she could follow difficult arguments. The fact is, when it came to any serious matter, she had the attention span of a child. He called her a disaster as a tenant. She cleaned up only under protest, ate whatever was around, wore anything she wanted, no respect for others, sweetly apologized when scolded, but didn't alter her behavior. Even in a Communist household there had to be a sense of propriety. "We did not know who would be there when we came home from work. A Norwegian? a Pole? an Englishman? an American? She organized her own League of Nations."

I told them she was great with me.

"Everyone loved Marishka," Annie said. "I was not so

< 222 >

angry as Bernard, but even he adored her. *Une belle fille,* but very young."

I said in this war I had many comrades. I would perhaps never again live so intimately with men. We had been necessary to each other, but the war was over and there was no longer any need for us to be together, so we were again strangers. With Marishka I had felt unguarded and joyful. The silly, immature, young woman—their irresponsible tenant—had eased my heart.

Bernard said, "Good for Marishka. She did her work well."

"You are fortunate to be so romantic," Annie said, meaning, I think, that she considered me inexperienced and without judgment.

They told me I might find Marishka with her mother in Haut Cagnes on the Côte d'Azur. Travel wasn't easy and they didn't know what transport was available.

I must have seemed naive, but more intelligent than they had thought. Bernard suggested we have a drink together at the Deux Magots the next afternoon. I said I was returning to my unit the next day. The fact is, I yearned for home and didn't intend any trip to the south of France.

I walked down to the Seine, sat on a bench, reread Dad's last letter. The tone had the oratorical, formal quality he had developed to cover his problems with ordinary language. The script was awkward, the letters wavering, his thick fingers and heavy hand better adapted to making fists than writing.

< 223 >

We are victorious, and you, my son, who were in the front lines of this great battle are safe. There will be festivities to celebrate your return. Your mother, like myself, is eager to embrace you. She will serve you a meal direct from her victory garden (photo enclosed.) We are very proud of you. We love you very much.

Despite three years of service and a stint of combat, I didn't feel wiser or braver or more mature.

I wrote him, describing how the war had ended, like all the war movies at the Dexter Theater, like all the hokey Hollywood scripts, like all my dreams of war. Justice done, the good guys ending with the beautiful girls and the loot, the bad guys dead or humbled. I asked, Did this mean there was a grand scriptwriter who saw to it that his chosen peoples would only be brought to the brink of extermination and then, in the manner of a commonplace action flick and at the last possible moment, be pulled back from the edge so that they might suffer once again through other cliff-hangers?

Not said in those terms, not so mocking. I thought it was my father I mocked with his simple scenarios and easy judgments about good guys and bad guys. But I only expressed my own yearning for simplicity.

Maurice once told me, no one is simple. And he meant there were no simple moral identifications, no clear distinctions between winners and losers, the quick and the dead. And I think he meant that the only possibility for joy in life was to give up simplicity, to give up one's faith in

< 224 >

unreal scenarios that precisely located us on some ladder of moral worth.

But in Paris, full of dreams of home, our war seemed to have confirmed simplicity. We had survived evil with the promise of a clear itinerary for the rest of the journey, advancing from one landmark to the next, ending far from any battleground, safe with our Bettys and Dottys and Sylvies, telling children our stories of war.

I wanted to strip away any evidence of war. The uniform would go. I would keep my camera. I would give my Luger to Dad. I would dispose of any other loot in my duffel bag and return home brand new.

What did Leo want?

I wanted everything to be simple.

I didn't ever again want to hear rockets or be summoned to give aid. I didn't ever again want to dig in or see anyone wounded or suffer anyone's dying.

We had been part of a system, spread over the world, organized in theaters and armies and corps and divisions and regiments and battalions and companies. We had had an exact address. We could locate ourselves down to platoon and squad. Now I wanted us to be scattered and never reassembled. No more armies or divisions or regiments or battalions or companies or platoons. No more theaters of war. No veterans' groups, no reunions, no visits to old battlefields, no celebration of what we once were compelled to be. Let that all be in the past, cleansed by recollection.

< 225 >